Stop Press

The last few weeks leading to the release of this book have been rather tumultuous for the financial services sector in India. It began with the 'Yes Bank' crisis that resulted in huge losses to the investors. The 'Infrastructure Leasing and Financial Services' (IL&FS) catastrophe followed—no one really saw it coming just as was the case with Lehman Brothers in the U.S. subprime (2007/8)—and a clear picture is yet to emerge on the havoc likely to be caused by this fiasco.

The latest development, as at the time of going to press, was the issuance of a Reserve Bank of India notice to 'Bandhan Bank' and the plummeting of its stock as a consequence. On October 1, 2018, Bandhan Bank's share value fell to Rs 452.20—down 20% (or by a whopping Rs 113.05) in a single day—adversely impacting its retail and institutional investors as also other stakeholders. Come December 2018, 'Kotak Bank' may well suffer the same fate as 'Bandhan Bank', if it fails to adhere to RBI norms for promoter shareholdings with regard to licensed banks. Add to the above, the 'Punjab National Bank' letter of understanding scam of 2018 and also the alleged conflicts of interest probe that is ongoing at 'ICICI Bank' and what we have is a serious crisis of faith in India's financial sector.

History continues to repeat itself. Solutions exist but it appears that no one is listening. First, the revolving door and reverse revolving door phenomenon must be stopped with regard to the financial services sector. Second, conflicts of interest must be identified and managed effectively. Third, good governance policies must be put into practice in real time—they should not gather dust on shelves in boardrooms. Fourth, internal audits must become truly independent. Last but not the least, good practices in the governance of compensation and governance of risk management must be upheld in all situations, especially the worst of times.

When will the captains of the financial sector learn from past crisis? Is it not smarter to learn (vicariously) from other peoples' mistakes? There are lessons a plenty but time is running out! Without a doubt, we need to put an end to financial crisis situations as they deter financial inclusion and contribute to financial exclusion. To achieve this, we must adopt a sound and practical financial inclusion paradigm as espoused in this book. And only if we do that, can we achieve the target of 100% sustained financial inclusion by 2030 as envisioned by the United Nations Sustainable Development Goal 1.3. And make no mistake—powering a billion dreams or more is certainly contingent on achieving the above milestone of 100% (sustained) financial inclusion, which is no less than a fundamental right.

Powering A Billion Dreams

Ramesh S Arunachalam

First published in October 2018 by
Shruthikka Media World

Copyright © 2018 Ramesh S Arunachalam.

Ramesh S Arunachalam has the complete moral right to be identified as author of this work, which presents his original ideas, analysis and writings.

Contact: shruthika438@gmail.com

Editing: Jyotirmoy Chaudhuri
Cover Design: K Ravindran
Research Assistance: SP Pandyan

Copyright Information

Ramesh S Arunachalam claims copyright only with the original writings, ideas, interpretation, and analysis done by the author, Ramesh S Arunachalam. No copyright is claimed with regard to any material that is cited or quoted—which are very negligible anyways (see appendix 5). In fact, 99% of the book comprises of original thoughts, ideas and analysis.

Dedication

This book is dedicated to my mother, Jaya Arunachalam and my mentor, Brij Mohan—two people, who have given their life and soul to the field of financial inclusion and empowerment.

Contents

Introduction	1
Chapter 1: Conflicts of Interest	13
Chapter 2: Causes for the Past Financial Crisis Situations	32
Chapter 3: Financial Inclusion, Towards Accountable Progress	43
Chapter 4: Financial Inclusion, Salient Issues	66
Chapter 5: Blockchains, What They Can Do for Financial Inclusion	84
Chapter 6: FinTech, Digitization and Digital Divide	106
Chapter 7: Financial Inclusion and Agriculture	117
Chapter 8: Value Chain Finance Can Power a Billion Dreams!	136
Chapter 9: Good Governance Critical For Sustained Financial Inclusion	147

Contents

Chapter 10: Governance of Compensation Necessary for Preventing Financial Exclusion — 161

Chapter 11: Governance of Risk Management Imperative to Prevent Financial Exclusion — 177

Chapter 12: Independent Internal Audits, the Key to Responsible Financial Inclusion Services — 188

Chapter 13: Customer Protection, the Key to Sustained Financial Inclusion — 196

Chapter 14: RegTech, the Key to Proactive Regulation and Supervision — 210

Chapter 15: Regulatory Accountability Vital for Sustained Financial Inclusion — 219

Conclusion — 231

Appendices — 248

Introduction

Finance is one of the most important resources in the world. There is hardly anything that you can do without money. That is why a healthy financial sector is so crucial for the development of the world, and also individual countries.

What constitutes a healthy financial sector? First and foremost, a healthy financial sector is one which is financially stable. In this context, financial stability means that financial intermediaries, markets and market infrastructure ensure the seamless flow of funds between savers and investors and thereby help facilitate growth in economic activity. Alternatively, a financial system can be deemed to be stable when it is able to perform its core functions—of financial intermediation, transmission of payments, pricing of financial instruments and risk allocation—in a smooth, efficient and effective manner. Additionally, the risk-bearing capacity of major financial institutions as well as financial infrastructure ought to be sufficient to withstand (if necessary) the severest of shocks and disruptions in the external environment.

While financial stability is a key aspect in defining a healthy financial sector, that alone is not enough. In today's world, a healthy financial sector would also need to be inclusive—one where all of its (mutually exclusive) citizens (irrespective of ethnicity, class, caste, religion, language, age, gender, region etc) have ongoing equal opportunities to gain access to a wide range of need-based, non-subsidized, affordable financial services, delivered in a customer friendly, convenient and transparent manner.

Indeed, it is to ensure the above that the United Nations (UN) set up the sustainable development goals[1] (SDGs) with SDG 1 standing for a world free of poverty by the year 2030. SDG 1 has as its sub-goal SDG 1.3, which calls for 100% (sustained[2]) financial inclusion by the year 2030.

While the SDGs are important steps in the right direction, what is really unfortunate is that no real tangible action is being taken towards measuring progress with regard to SDG 1.3—especially, in terms of the total (physical head count) number of

---

[1] For a contextual explanation with regard to the sustainable development goal 1, see the following:
http://www.undp.org/content/undp/en/home/sustainable-development-goals/goal-1-no-poverty.html

[2] The concept of financial inclusion is a very dynamic one, whereby, people can get included, excluded, re-included and so on. Therefore, a correct interpretation of SDG 1.3 would come to mean that, by 2030, every mutually exclusive individual is financially included and stays included—this is what I call "sustained" financial inclusion.

mutually exclusive individuals[3] (worldwide) who have been financially included (and who remain included thereafter).

Despite billions of dollars of taxpayers' money and private resources being routed towards achieving 100% financial inclusion, there is no one in this world who can give us a population-based estimate of the number of mutually exclusive individuals who are financially included at any specific instance (globally as well as by country), across all types of financial inclusion services, or for that matter by an individual financial inclusion service.[4]

---

[3] Currently, there are several (inadequate) attempts that estimate the level of financial inclusion using (small) sample surveys. Some of the key demand-side data sources that estimate levels of financial inclusion are: 1) The Global Findex; 2) The FinScope Survey; 3) FinAccess/Access to Financial Services Surveys; 4) Financial Inclusion Tracker Surveys (FITS); and 5) Financial Inclusion Insight Surveys (FII). Likewise, some of the supply-side data sources that estimate levels of financial inclusion are: 1) The IMF Financial Access Survey (FAS); 2) GSMA Mobile Money Adoption Survey; 3) World Bank's Global Payment Systems Survey; and 4) The MIX's Geospatial Maps. For reasons outlined in this book (particularly, chapters 3 and 4), these well-meaning efforts are inadequate in tracking progress towards SDG 1.3.

[4] Sample surveys like the Global Findex survey are of no real use when it comes to measuring a dynamic construct like financial inclusion in a reliable and valid manner. Sample surveys offer just a snapshot of this very dynamic construct, financial inclusion, based on (so-called) representational data. They are not at all suitable for measuring progress towards 100% financial inclusion as per SDG 1.3. This is because financial inclusion is dynamic in nature and the excluded can be financially included but there is nothing to prevent them from being financially excluded again. History is replete with examples of this arrangement of musical chairs that see people entering and exiting the financial system in a jiffy. So, we need accurate population (universe and not sample) estimates of mutually exclusive individuals who are financially included at any instance. See

This is indeed a very sad state of affairs. If we cannot provide an accurate estimate with regard to the number of mutually exclusive people who are financially included at any instance, anywhere, (globally and by country), what is the use of all those high-flying projects that are being implemented with regard to financial inclusion as well as its measurement? How will we know whether these projects have had any impact or benefit at all—at least in so far as their ability to financially include excluded people and help them stay included thereafter. How will we know whether mutually exclusive people previously excluded (in a financial sense) are now being financially included and whether mutually excluded individuals previously included (in a financial sense) are now being financially excluded?

Furthermore, unless we know exactly what is the quality and level of financial inclusion today (i.e., where we are today), how can we devise strategies to get to where we want to be by 2030—i.e., where all mutually exclusive individuals[5] worldwide are financially included. And unless we have measures that can help us continuously track progress towards SDGs, how can we know as to whether we are travelling in the right direction?

---

chapter 4 for a comprehensive explanation of this. As noted above, the existing small sample survey-based efforts to measure financial inclusion are, at best, inadequate.

[5] We are primarily talking about adults here—i.e., people above the age of 18 or as applicable from country to country—although parents or guardians can access financial services for and on behalf of their (minor) children, for education, insurance and so on.

Powering A Billion Dreams

Let us leave this aside for a moment.

I have a basic question!

When is someone financially included? When they have a savings bank (zero balance) account and yet do not operate it at all (or at best, use it once in a while)? Or when they have accessed a loan, whose basic terms and conditions themselves result in their not being able to repay the loan (see the case of the sugarcane farmers discussed later in the book) or when they send money back to their family or relatives using a very expensive remittance service (say once every 6 months) or when they access an insurance service and stop paying premiums after they are told they are ineligible for a payout or when they contribute to a pension fund for their old age security that is long way off, and so on?

The point that I am trying to make here is that, despite all these billions of dollars invested into financial inclusion, we still have no globally and universally accepted definition of financial inclusion—one that is sound enough to lend itself to real time measurement and also one that is adaptive enough to reflect reality in different contextual situations globally. Here I am talking of financial inclusion, which is highly dynamic in nature and operates as a cycle, whereby people get included, excluded, re-included, excluded and so on.

Yet another aspect needs to be highlighted here. A lot of financial innovation has been taking place after 2004 and 2005 and much of it concerns the use of financial products and processes to help (financially) include excluded people.

While financial innovation is crucial, unfortunately, in the name of financial innovation, frauds and scams can occur—the U.S. subprime of 2007/8 or the Indian microfinance crisis in Andhra Pradesh (AP) of 2010 are cases in point here. A second issue that concerns financial innovation is the fact that oftentimes, arguments are made that for real innovation to occur, regulatory ease (or regulatory handicap[6]) is required. This often manifests itself in financial companies either choosing the weakest financial sector regulator or having their regulatory requirements 'eased' and made 'flexible' through lobbying—both of which result in unbridled, relentless growth in financial services and poor practices in corporate governance, service delivery and internal controls (for these financial services) in real time. Not just that, conflicts of interest also rear their ugly head and the net result are scams and frauds, of the kind we have encountered in the last decade starting with the U.S. subprime (2007/8).

In fact, in all these scams and frauds, corporate governance, and the role of independent directors, has been called into question because of serious conflicts of interest. So, a key point that I am trying to make here is that conflicts of interest in the

---

[6] A regulatory handicap in the financial sector manifests itself in several ways: a) It results in easing of regulatory requirements for the concerned class of entities; b) It reduces legal compliances for these entities; c) It forsakes accountability from a regulatory standpoint.

financial sector, especially, in the regulatory domain,[7] led to innovation going astray and ultimately resulted in the end users suffering—be it the U.S. subprime (2007/8), the Indian microfinance crisis (2010) in AP, or the more recent U.S. $ 2 billion scam in the Punjab National Bank in 2018.

Given the above context, this book attempts to take a close look at the financial sector and isolate issues related to it that could undermine our efforts towards a world free of poverty by 2030 (as per SDG 1) and a world where there is 100% (sustained) financial inclusion, where people once financially included remain that way thereafter.

To this end, the remainder of this book is structured as follows:

Chapter 1 looks at one of the most important yet neglected constructs in the financial sector—a construct that could seriously undermine our efforts in reaching our goal of a world free of poverty (by 2030, as per SDG 1) and its sub-goal of 100% (sustained) financial inclusion by 2030. This chapter thus defines the critical construct of 'conflicts of

---

[7] Conflicts of interest have been the bane of the financial sector but what is critical is to note the fact that when they permeate the regulatory domain, then the very axle on which the wheels of the financial sector spin become weak and subject to a huge torque—this results in the axle breaking, causing tremendous turmoil. This is what happened in the U.S. subprime (2007/8) or the 2010 Indian microfinance crisis (AP) or, for that matter, the recent Indian banking crisis of 2018 where the U.S. 2 billion-dollar scam at Punjab National Bank (PNB) and huge non-performing asset (NPA) crisis (at other banks) leads the way.

interest' and shows how it led to past scams and frauds, all the while re-emphasizing the fact that, unless identified and managed appropriately (and on time), conflicts of interest could derail the financial inclusion express that is currently being turbocharged with multiple engines by many stakeholders, including central banks.

Chapter 2 goes on to dissect past crisis situations—especially the U.S. subprime of 2007/8 and the Indian microfinance crisis of 2010 in AP as well as the recent (2018) banking scams and frauds[8]—in order to isolate the key factors that led to these scams and frauds in the first place. This is to enable us to control all of these critical factors in the future and thereby prevent large-scale scams and frauds from occurring in the larger financial sector. Any further scams will distract us from achieving 100% sustained financial inclusion by 2030 and, therefore, it is important to understand past financial sector failures—especially, the U.S. subprime (2007/8) and the Indian microfinance crisis in AP (2010)—and 'secure' and safeguard the financial sector from further scams and frauds that could derail us in a systemic sense. The U.S. subprime fiasco and the Indian microfinance crisis are very important because, in a way, they pertained to low income and excluded people in the financial sector.

Chapter 3 focuses on preventing ambiguity in defining, operationalizing and measuring financial inclusion. It goes on to talk about 'where we are

---

[8] This includes the recent U.S. $ 2 billion scam at Punjab National Bank in 2018.

today' with regard to the construct of (sustained) financial inclusion, especially in relation to SDG 1.3. The chapter talks about the dynamic nature of financial inclusion—whereby people get included, excluded, re-included all the time—and provides real life examples of the same. It then proposes that mere financial inclusion cannot help—what is required is sustained financial inclusion, whereby people once financially included stay included thereafter. It also describes the basic framework for measuring financial inclusion, so that we can track, in real time, the progress towards 100% (sustained) financial inclusion by 2030.

Chapter 4 outlines salient issues that need to be kept in mind with regard to financial inclusion, especially in relation to reaching our goal of 100% (sustained) financial inclusion by 2030. As argued in the chapter, we need to keep (our) focus on these issues while tracking accountable progress towards SDG 1.3.

Chapters 5, 6, 7 and 8 look at what kinds of innovation—in financial products, processes and organizations—are required to not only ensure 100% (sustained) financial inclusion by 2030 but also to empower at least a billion people to realize their dreams. There is a special focus on the much neglected agricultural sector (which is still in crisis today) and micro, small and medium enterprises (MSMEs), which form the backbone of the economic growth of many countries. Most importantly, key insights are provided with regard to how digitization, FinTech[9] and blockchains[10] can play a real role in empowering at least a billion people to realize their dreams.

Chapters 9, 10 and 11 deal with the crucial aspect of governance, risk management and compensation in traditional and new age financial institutions—all with a view to ensuring accountable, transparent and fair delivery of traditional and new age financial services by a wide variety of traditional and eclectic financial institutions in such a manner that financial crisis situations (like the U.S. subprime of 2007/8 and Indian microfinance crisis of 2010) do not occur and 100% sustained financial inclusion by 2030 becomes a reality in accordance with SDG 1.3.

Chapter 12 adds on to the above by emphasizing the immense value of designing and putting in place independent internal audits—which can be the first

---

[9] FinTech usually refers to use of technology for delivering financial services. A simple example is a digital wallet and there are many more artificial intelligence based technology applications for design and delivery of financial services. All these come under the realm of FinTech.

[10] A blockchain is an open distributed ledger that fundamentally acts as a database of financial, legal, physical or electronic assets that can be shared across a network of multiple sites, geographies or institutions. The most wonderful aspect is that all participants within the network have their own identical copy of the ledger. And any changes to the ledger are reflected in all copies—at the earliest within seconds and at the latest within minutes. The security and accuracy of the various assets in the ledger are maintained cryptographically through the use of 'keys' and signatures—this is to control who can perform what actions within the shared ledger. Entries can also be updated by one, some, or all of the participants, according to rules agreed by the network, which often has multi-stakeholder governance.

line of defense that any financial institution has with regard to fraud, conflicts of interest, corruption and the like, which have been elaborately highlighted in chapters 2 and 3. The reason for avoiding fraud, conflicts of interest and corrupt practices in financial service delivery is because in the end they result in the very exclusion of the people we want to include in the first place.

Chapter 13 looks at the crucial aspect of consumer protection—a construct very much in demand but very much ignored, as is evident from an analysis of past scams, frauds and financial crisis situations. It outlines a pragmatic strategy with regard to consumer protection, especially with regard to financial and digital financial inclusion.

Chapters 14 and 15 look at the regulatory and supervisory domain. While chapter 14 looks at the use of technology[11] for regulation and supervision to enhance its effectiveness and efficiency, besides getting early warning signals of impending financial crisis, chapter 15 looks at the all-important construct of governance and articulates the kind of (systemic) changes that regulators will have to undergo for our goal of 100% sustained financial inclusion to be achieved by 2030. Aspects covered by this chapter include the management of conflicts of interest, governance of compensation, governance of risk management and the like—mainly for regulators and supervisors.

---

[11] The use of technology for regulation and supervision is often called as RegTech.

Chapter 16 is the concluding chapter which summarizes the key strategic action steps going forward—both from a macro as well as micro perspective—for achieving the laudable goal of 100% sustained financial inclusion by 2030 and thereby empowering a billion dreams, if not more.

One final word before I close this introduction. The book uses practical knowledge from the field coupled with an eclectic design thinking framework to analyze problems and create flexible solutions (based on insight and empathy) within a larger ecosystem. This is bound to ensure success, with a higher degree of certainty. Done this way, 100% sustained financial inclusion will, as Steve Jobs often said, 'wow' the end-user customer and help contribute to building a world free of poverty and a world with 100% sustained financial inclusion by 2030, where more than a billion dreams can surely be realized!

Chapter 1

Conflicts of Interest

Let us look back at some of the key financial sector scams and frauds that have caught public attention over the last decade, as they can distract us from our desired goal of 100% financial inclusion by 2030 as per SDG 1.3. This is because such frauds and scams can sometimes exacerbate the impact of regulation—frequently, as an immediate response to a crisis (which often occurs because there has been a regulatory failure), regulation suddenly becomes very rigid and thereby starts to stifle genuine growth and innovation, both of which are necessary for enhancing inclusiveness in the global financial sector.

Getting back to the financial sector scams, some of the key ones[1] in the last ten years include: the 2018 Punjab National Bank (PNB) U.S. $ 2 billion scam caused by the fake and fraudulent letters of understanding (LoUs), the Indian microfinance crisis of 2010 in Andhra Pradesh (AP), the erstwhile Satyam Computers finance and accounting fraud of 2009, and the U.S. subprime crisis of 2007/8.

Now, if you ignore—from the above list—the erstwhile Satyam Computers accounting fraud of 2009, which also had its fair share of finance and accounting related aspects, all of the other examples fall completely within the realm of the financial services sector. That is not all! Several of these past crisis situations have another common thread among their many antecedents, which is the fact that they all resulted because a regulatory and supervisory failure occurred in the financial services sector. Put differently, had the regulatory and supervisory frameworks for the financial services sector functioned effectively, then I am quite certain that many of these crisis situations could have been completely avoided, or at least nipped in the bud.

In fact, if there is one thing that stands out about these financial crisis situations, it is the fact that weak, lax and laissez-faire regulatory frameworks[2]—

---

[1] This list is by no means exhaustive.
[2] As far as the financial services sector is concerned, regulation denotes the rules aimed at financial institutions and govern their functioning. The primary objective in regulation is to: a) ensure financial stability; b) protect actual users of financial services; and c) facilitate (sustained) inclusivity, whereby citizens (irrespective of ethnicity, race, gender, age, religion, class, caste, region, etc) gain

14

often caused by conflicts of interest at various levels, lobbying, campaign financing, and the power of Wall Street, banks and financial institutions to influence policy makers, regulators and others—served as an important factor that triggered the crisis in the first place.[3]

What makes it very interesting is the fact that many of these frameworks were either developed by industry insiders with commercial interests or created with significant input from such insiders—both with a view to benefit the overall financial industry concerned and pretend that everything is okay when, in fact, things were going horribly wrong!

The above should not be taken lightly because it clearly suggests that conflicts of interest were at play in several domains, including regulatory and supervisory ones. In other words, when all these crisis situations took place, serious conflicts of

---

ongoing access to need-based, non-subsidized, affordable financial services delivered in a customer-friendly and transparent manner. Overseeing and ensuring compliance with the above rules (i.e., regulation) is the responsibility of supervisors. While the regulator and supervisor could be one and the same institution like the central bank, they could also be different entities. For example, in the case of commercial banks in India, the Reserve Bank of India (RBI) is the regulator as well as supervisor, whereas for the cooperative banks, RBI is the regulator and the National Bank for Agriculture and Rural Development (NABARD) is the supervisor.

[3] See for example, the 'Financial Crisis Inquiry Report, Final Report of the National Commission on the Causes of the Financial and Economic Crisis in the United States', The Financial Crisis Inquiry Commission, 2011. Similar writings exist with regard to the Indian microfinance crisis of 2010 in Andhra Pradesh. See appendix 1 for details of books, papers and articles written by Ramesh S Arunachalam in this regard.

interest led to lax and laissez-faire regulatory and supervisory frameworks and approaches being developed in the first place. And what is really interesting is that industry insiders (or those closely linked to them) were playing an important role in setting the norms for regulating and supervising their very own industry—the financial services sector.

While a lot of this can be attributed to the revolving door and reverse revolving door phenomena that has now existed for a long time, there can be no doubt that this was corruption at its worst, caused by inherent conflicts of interests that were at play. Thus, it would not be an overstatement to argue that these conflicts of interest (at various levels and places) were themselves a key cause for these different crisis situations. Much of the above continues even today in the financial sector, and I am re-emphasizing the conflicts of interest aspect again because it is an area of significant importance, especially for regulators.

And this is something that central banks and other financial service regulators need to note with urgency because if not identified and eliminated (or at least managed prudently), such conflicts of interest could spell disaster for the larger financial sector again. Mind you, unlike in 2007/8, today's financial institutions are much larger, more risky and, therefore, could cause greater devastation (if and when things go wrong). And this effort is a means to record the above warning publicly and suggest several ways by which regulation and supervision of the financial sector can devoid itself of conflicts of interest.

Strangely, despite all that has happened in the last decade, even today, there is a puzzling lack of attention given to the role played by conflicts of interest in the corruption saga and especially with regard to the larger financial sector. Look at the United Nations Convention against Corruption (UNCAC). Even the UNCAC only makes a fleeting mention of the role played by conflicts of interests, despite it being an important keystone to unearthing corruption and supporting the structure to fight against corruption worldwide.

It is not just my opinion; many scholars, academics, economists, politicians, and business people worldwide also agree that close regulation and monitoring of conflicts of interest are of great importance to regulatory ethics. Moreover, this is something that all of us need to note with urgency because, if not eliminated, these conflict of interest situations could spell disaster for the larger financial sector, as they will inevitably lead to corruption and, ultimately, to financial crisis caused by laissez-faire and/or vested interest-led regulation and supervision—the most recent case of the PNB U.S. $ 2 billion scam being a great example of how much damage conflicts of interest can do in real time with regard to the important functions of internal audit, concurrent audit and banking supervision, all of which failed to unearth the scam early in its occurrence.

Having set the broad context, let us now look at what is meant by 'conflicts of interest.'

In very basic and simple terms, a conflict of interest is a scenario where a person or firm has an incentive to serve one's (own) interest at the expense of another's interest. For example, this might denote serving the interest of the company (firm or institution) over that of a client and/or serving the interest of one set of institutions and their clients over another set of institutions and clients.

Why attach so much importance to conflicts of interest with regard to regulation and supervision in the financial sector? This is because if it is not entirely eliminated and/or at least properly managed/reduced, conflicts of interest can even threaten the entire financial system, its financial stability, inclusiveness, and so on. As noted above, this is what past crises situations clearly tell us. In fact, if there is a single most recurring theme in financial crises and scandals globally, it is the failure to identify and appropriately manage conflicts of interest.

While some relevant (non-exhaustive) examples of conflicts of interest are given later, let us now try and define conflicts of interest more precisely, especially as it relates to institutions in the regulatory and supervisory domain of the financial sector. A 'conflict of interest' is a conflict between the duty, roles, responsibilities, and private interests of any official (including those who regulate/supervise the financial sector) that could improperly and unfairly influence the performance of his/her official roles and responsibilities.

By private interests, I mean the following: Private interests include financial, pecuniary and other interests[4] which generate a direct personal benefit to the public official, including personal affiliations, associations, and family ties, that could be considered as likely to improperly and unfairly influence the official's performance of his/her roles, duties and responsibilities, especially in the regulatory and supervisory domain.

Defined in this way, conflict of interest has the potential to undermine the proper functioning of all institutions[5] (public, private, not-for-profit, joint sector etc), governments and the like by:

- Weakening adherence by officials to the ideals of impartiality, objectivity, fairness, and legitimacy in decision making, and
- Distorting the rule of law, the development and application of policy, the functioning of organizations and markets, as well as the allocation of resources.

At this juncture, it is crucial to point out the difference between conflicts of interest and corruption.

---

[4] The negotiation of future employment by an official (for himself/family/friends) prior to his leaving his present office is one example, and there are many more examples that I could provide. This is like negotiating a job with a vendor. For example, an official may say, "I will make rules governing X and Y situations very lenient provided you make my nephew the CEO in another project of yours."

[5] This would include regulators and supervisors.

Conflict of interest situations exist where officials (including those in the regulatory/supervisory domain), because of their position, have the *opportunity* to abuse the power and authority of their position for personal and private gain. On the other hand, corruption exists where officials *have abused* their position for personal and private gain. Put differently, conflict of interest situations do not always lead to corruption. However, where there is corruption, you can be sure that conflicts of interest indeed exist.

Why do we need to attach so much importance to conflicts of interest with regard to regulation and supervision in the financial sector?

This is because if conflicts of interest are not eliminated and/or at least properly identified and managed, as noted earlier, the situation can easily lead to corruption in regulation and supervision and thereby threaten the entire financial system, its stability, inclusiveness and so on. This is not new. This is what past crisis situations have taught us repeatedly. In fact, if there is a single most recurring theme in financial crises and scandals globally, it is the failure to identify and manage conflicts of interest—something that we have chosen to ignore until now.

The following are some well-known examples from the United States and India and they provide very useful learning with regard to conflicts of interest and their relationship to weak regulatory and supervisory systems, especially in crisis situations. They hold very important lessons for financial sector regulators and supervisors worldwide—many of whom seem to be embarking on a very dangerous journey in their effort to turbocharge financial inclusion and grow the financial sector in a tearing hurry.

In the United States, starting with the 1929 market crash, bank involvement in the securities markets came under close scrutiny. The famous Pecora hearings of 1933 that focused on the reasons of the 1929 market crash and the resultant banking crisis showcased a whole range of abusive strategies used by banks and bank affiliates. It is important to note that these included a multitude of conflicts of interest—the underwriting of unsound securities to pay off bad bank loans and 'pool operations' to support the price of bank stocks are two such examples.[6] And of course, the regulatory and supervisory system of the day was a mere observer.

In fact, as has been argued,[7] it is the significant revelations of "uncontrolled conflicts of interest" that provided the basis and rationale for strengthening of the extant regulatory framework by the passing of many subsequent regulations—the Securities Act (1933), the Securities Exchange Act (1934), and the Glass-Steagall Banking Act (1933). Conflicts of interest also appear to be the major reason for the enactment of the Investment

---

[6] See the testimony of Arthur Levitt, Chairman U.S. Securities and Exchange Commission,
https://www.sec.gov/news/testimony/testarchive/1995/spch029.txt
[7] Ibid.

Company Act (1940) and the Investment Advisor Act (1940).

Closer to the 1990s, when I lived in the United States for several years, I personally saw numerous examples of conflicts of interest leading to a crisis, especially because of a lax regulatory system dominated by conflicts of interest:

- The insider trading scandals (such as the Ivan Boesky and Dennis Levine scandals in the 1980s), the closure of Drexel Burnham Lambert (the investment bank) and the associated (criminal) conviction of its famous employee (Michael Milken) are still fresh in my memory.
- And then there were more financial scandals in the early 2000s—for example, the internet bubble in 2000/2001 exposed problems with dubious high-flying research analysts (with very significant conflicts of interest) whose reports were in fact influenced by their own institutions' investment banking interests. This, in fact, led to specific provisions in the Sarbanes-Oxley Act that dealt with conflicts of interest among research analysts.
- And just about a decade ago, in 2003, the U.S. Securities and Exchange Commission (SEC) found that the use of brokerage commissions to facilitate the sales of fund shares [was] widespread among funds that relied on broker-dealers to sell fund shares. This led to the adoption of new rules to prohibit funds from this practice.[8]

---

[8] Please see http://www.sec.gov/rules/final/ic-26591.pdf— Prohibition on the Use of Brokerage Commissions to Finance

And then, we had the mother of all financial crises in recent times—the global financial crisis of 2007/8, which was again based on significant conflicts of interest in many areas such as the production and sale of mortgage-backed securities, the rating of these instruments, and so on.

As noted in the report[9] of the Financial Crisis Inquiry Commission (FCIC), conflicts of interest that existed among rating agencies in evaluating collateralized debt obligation (CDO) deals was investigated by the SEC which subsequently issued a report in June 2008 that stated that conflicts of interest at Moody's was indeed a major issue. And interestingly, this report argues that structured finance was the mechanism used by credit rating agencies (whose own motives were hugely conflicted) to convert subprime and other mortgages into complex investments with triple-A ratings. Interestingly, this market relied on precise computer models—that were completely divorced from reality—and on ever-increasing housing prices. When that bubble finally burst, the complexity bubble also ruptured: the securities that almost no one ever comprehended, backed by mortgages that no lender would have signed two decades ago, were the first dominoes to fall in the financial sector.

Distribution, Investment Company Act Release 26591 (Sept. 2, 2004), 69 Fed. Register 54728, 54728 (Sept. 9, 2004).

[9] 'Financial Crisis Inquiry Report, Final Report of the National Commission on the Causes of the Financial and Economic Crisis in the United States', The Financial Crisis Inquiry Commission, 2011, http://fcic-static.law.stanford.edu/cdn_media/fcic-reports/fcic_final_report_full.pdf

Yet, no regulator was serious enough to take action in time to prevent this gaffe. If you ask me why, I would say it was due to conflicts of interest in the regulatory domain—sometimes due to the revolving door policy and the reverse revolving door phenomenon. Just as an aside, I would like to state there are huge problems with securitization in the microfinance sector as well (globally) and these continue even today.

Getting back to the FCIC report, it cited several other conflicts underlying the crisis such as: a) underwriters assisting CDO managers in selecting collateral; and b) hedge fund managers selecting collateral from their funds to place in CDOs that they offered to other investors. According to the FCIC report, in the above connection, the SEC investigated the rating agencies' ratings of mortgage-backed securities and CDOs in 2007 and reported its findings in July 2008. The SEC criticized Moody's for several aspects: a) not verifying the accuracy of mortgage information; b) leaving that responsibility to due diligence firms and other stakeholders; c) not retaining (key) documentation about how many of the deals were rated; d) knowingly permitting the quality of ratings to be compromised by the nature and complexity of the CDO deals; e) not having the requisite staff to rate the CDOs; f) flushing ratings out with inadequate review; g) not adequately disclosing information about the rating process for mortgage-backed securities and CDOs; and h) most importantly, letting conflicts of interest affect the rating decisions.

Yet another conflict cited in the report was about Citigroup offering "liquidity puts" that gave it significant fees in the short term but placed significant financial risk on it in the long term. The FCIC report noted that there was a potential conflict of interest in pricing the liquidity so that more CDO equities could be sold and a lot more structuring fees could be generated—the report also argued that this resulted in such severe losses that it might have brought the huge financial conglomerate to the brink of failure.

Another high profile example of conflict of interest in recent years is the settlement that the SEC reached with Goldman Sachs, in which the firm paid $ 550 million to settle charges filed by the Commission, and acknowledged that disclosures made in marketing a subprime mortgage product contained incomplete information, as they did not disclose the role of a hedge fund client who was taking the opposite side of the trade in the selection of the CDO.

And as the Honorable Court documents note,[10] Goldman Sachs acknowledged that incomplete information was contained in the marketing materials for the ABACUS 2007-AC1 transaction. Especially, it

---

[10] Paraphrased from documents (Page 2, point 3) of The United States District Court Southern District of New York, U.S. Securities and Exchange Commission, Plaintiff, Vs. Goldman, Sachs and Co. and Fabrice Tourre, Defendants, http://www.sec.gov/litigation/litreleases/2010/consent-pr2010-123.pdf

was agreed that it was a mistake for the Goldman Sachs marketing materials to state that the reference portfolio had been "selected by" ACA Management LLC without disclosing the role of Paulson & Co. Inc. in the portfolio selection process and also the fact that Paulson's economic interests were adverse to CDO investors. Goldman regretted that the marketing materials did not contain that disclosure.

After the 2007/8 financial crisis, there are a few examples of problems that arose from poorly controlled conflicts of interest coupled with lax regulatory frameworks. One is the famous case of Barclays Bank, which acknowledged misconduct related to *possible collusion* to artificially set LIBOR (London Interbank Offered Rate). As all of us know, LIBOR is a very significant benchmark that is used to set short-term interest rates on different financial instruments, including derivatives.

Another is the 2010 AP microfinance crisis which is again a classic example of the conflict of interest problem coupled with a weak regulatory framework! In the 2010 AP crisis, the lax regulation and laissez-faire supervision of the NBFC-MFIs[11] (done at the behest of the microfinance industry at large and NBFCs in particular and RBI's own misplaced trust in NBFC-MFIs as Dr YV Reddy, former Governor

---

[11] NBFC-MFIs is a category of NBFCs as per the central bank regulatory classification in India. NBFC = Non-Banking Finance Company and MFI = Microfinance Institution. The central bank in India is Reserve Bank of India (RBI). Non Bank Finance Institutions (NBFIs) are called as NBFCs in India.

has himself admitted[12]) led to the eventual crisis on the ground.

Likewise, in 2013, the conflicts of interests prevalent in the RBI financial inclusion committee were indeed very serious, as it had many members representing companies (institutions) that had significant commercial interest in the broad area of financial inclusion, including microfinance. Across the board, these members and the institutions therefore stood to benefit from the recommendations, regulatory or otherwise, made by this committee and that is exactly how things panned out later.[13]

What needs to be emphasized here is the fact that the *broad industry of financial inclusion,* which needs to be regulated (in an independent fashion) surely had no right to decide on its own regulation. In fact, many of the past crisis situations given above can be linked to lax and laissez-faire regulatory/supervisory frameworks that had either been developed by industry insiders with commercial interests and/or been created with significant input from such insiders—both with a view to benefit the overall industry concerned!

This is especially a key point to note because in the past, the RBI has had lots of committees comprising of microfinance industry insiders who decided on how to regulate and supervise themselves—this

---

[12] He has admitted this in his article in the *Economic and Political Weekly*. See appendix 2, the bibliography, for a listing of this article.
[13] See the articles by Ramesh S Arunachalam in *Moneylife* listed in appendix 1.

resulted in the Krishna district AP 2006 microfinance crisis, the Kolar 2009 localized microfinance crisis and the statewide 2010 AP microfinance crisis, to name a few.[14]

In fact, in 2013, when the above happened, I wrote, "protecting independent committees that are looking into regulation/supervision in the financial sector—*from the influence of the companies (institutions) operating in the same financial markets*—is a strong prerequisite to ensure the effectiveness of the regulatory architecture being developed. Otherwise, the threat arises that, instead of being guided by public and larger client interests, such committees (like the RBI financial inclusion committee) will promote the interests of the companies and institutions whose activities are supposed to be regulated and supervised. And the RBI can ignore this important fact concerning its own financial inclusion committee at its own peril!"

Moving on, in 2018, one of India's biggest bank frauds occurred, and it was allegedly carried out by Nirav Modi, Mehul Choksi and associates at PNB—it has been reported[15] that Nirav Modi and his uncle Mehul Choksi, in connivance with certain bank officials, allegedly cheated PNB of about Rs 14,000 crore (which is close to U.S. $ 2 billion) through issuance of fraudulent LoUs.[16] Specifically, a Mumbai

---

[14] All places named in this paragraph are situated in India.
[15] See appendix 2 for articles on the Punjab National Bank (2018) scam.
[16] A Letter of Undertaking (LoU) is like a bank guarantee under which a bank operating as per Reserve Bank of India norms can allow its customer to raise money from another Indian bank's branch (located abroad) in the form of short-term credit. The terms of

branch (Brady House) of PNB, just a short (walking) distance from the headquarters of India's central bank, had fraudulently issued over several hundred LoUs for the group of companies belonging to Nirav Modi since March 2011. Reports say that the exact number of LoUs issued to the companies of Nirav Modi, his relatives and the Nirav Modi Group were 1,213. Likewise, Mehul Choksi, his relatives and the Gitanjali Group were reportedly issued 377 LoUs. Here again, it appears that conflicts of interest[17] among bank officials at various levels of analysis—including its senior management, board of directors (comprising of independent and other directors who together were to safeguard the larger interests of the shareholders as well as the public) and internal and concurrent auditors—could have played a key role in perpetrating this whole fraud. And without a doubt, banking supervisors and a very lax regulatory and supervisory framework also have to carry the blame for this huge unprecedented U.S. $ 2 billion fraud.

A special comment is in order here. While providing regulatory directives for good corporate governance is always easy, ensuring good corporate governance is what has proven difficult, especially when conflicts of interest are at play. That is where independent directors have to play a proactive and catalytic role.

---

issuing the LoU generally include payment of margin money (to the bank issuing the LOU). The LoU may also have other contractual elements, like payment terms and so on and so forth. Issuance of LoUs has now been discontinued in India after the RBI mandated the same, vide its circular dated 2018.

[17] Only when the investigation by the Central Bureau of Investigation is completed will we know how the scam and fraud unfolded in its entirety.

In fact, the very premise of good corporate governance hinges on the ability of independent directors to act impartially, objectively and with prudence, keeping in mind the overall vision of the institution and its duty to all of its stakeholders (including shareholders, customers and others)—all the while ensuring that conflicts of interest do not hamper the transparent, effective *(doing the right things)* and efficient *(doing things the right way)* functioning of the institution.

You may wonder why I have placed so much of an onus on independent directors. One of the most critical reasons for the importance attached to independent directors in any organization relates to conflicts of interest. There are several issues here: (i) conflicts of interest hinder judgment and affect decision making; (ii) judgment and decision making are what directors are asked to do; and (iii) directors must feel free to think, express, question and decide in the interests of those they represent—the stakeholders (including shareholders, customers and others)—without conflicts of interest impacting their judgment and decision making. And independent directors are the only governance safeguards with regard to this and that is why they are mandatory in all kinds of organizations, including financial institutions (especially those that are systemically important).

And when independent directors fail to exercise their duty, as was the case in many of the institutions at the forefront of U.S. subprime crisis in 2007/8, the 2010 Indian microfinance crisis in AP, and the Indian banking crisis in 2018, conflicts of interest begin to raise their ugly head at all levels, including the regulatory domain, and the net result is not only scams and frauds at the institutional level but also, more importantly, a systemic failure at the regulatory and supervisory levels. Indeed, all of these crisis situations were the result of a multitude of factors and we take a close look at the causes of these crisis situations in the next chapter.

Chapter 2

Causes for the Past Financial Crisis Situations

As noted in chapter 1, it becomes important to delve deeper into the past financial crisis situations over the last decade and look at what happened and how it happened—only then, can we understand why things happened the way they did. Accordingly, this chapter is devoted to such analysis, whereby we also get to understand some of the key causes behind these financial crisis situations, especially the U.S. subprime (2007/8) and Indian microfinance crisis of 2010 in Andhra Pradesh (AP).

Understanding these causes is critical because in our desire to reach 100% sustained financial inclusion by 2030, we will be taking many more steps towards growth and innovation in the financial sector. While this growth and innovation is necessary for the desired 100% inclusivity, we must also tread carefully so that we don't repeat past mistakes—lest we get back to square one in terms of creating yet another crisis.

That said, let us move to understand some commonalities associated with these past crisis situations. The first aspect to note is that all of these crises situations were the result of human action as well as inaction—neither computer models nor algorithms had gone haywire. And of course, mother nature clearly had no role in these. I am saying all of this to re-emphasize the fact that all of these crisis situations were human made and, therefore, were completely avoidable.

To paraphrase Cassius who tells Brutus (in *Julius Caesar*), the fault did not lie in our stars but rather within us. Similarly, all of the financial crisis situations could have been avoided, had the so-called captains of the financial services industry and the public stewards of the larger financial system latched on to the early warning signals and initiated appropriate on-course corrections immediately. Sadly, that was not to be—indeed, theirs was not a mere missed step but rather a huge fall, for which we, the public and others (like shareholders, investors, employees, etc) have paid a heavy price.

In the U.S. subprime (2007/8), the explosion in risky subprime lending and securitization, a huge, unsustainable rise in housing prices, large-scale and widespread reports of aggressive and predatory lending, significant increases in mortgage debt, burgeoning growth in financial firms' trading activities—all of which were red flags—were all ignored, and no real action was taken on the ground to quell the various threats. In particular, the Federal Reserve's total failure in stemming the flow of toxic mortgages deserves mention. Indeed, the Federal Reserve was one entity that had the power to set prudent mortgage lending standards—yet it did not, for reasons known only to it.

Three basic actions by key stakeholders were ignored by the Federal Reserve and this was a huge miss—(a) financial institutions made, bought and sold mortgage securities that they either never examined or knew to be defective. The Federal Reserve did nothing at all about this; (b) huge borrowings (billions and billions of dollars) were the source of funds for many firms and these had to be renewed every night, often secured by subprime mortgages—yet nothing was done from a regulatory perspective; (c) most importantly, major firms and investors relied primarily and rather blindly on credit rating agencies (which had serious conflicts of interest) as arbiters of risk. Yet there was no one (especially from the regulatory side) looking at this blind faith on conflicted credit rating agencies.

In many ways, be it the unparalleled growth in mortgage securities or huge borrowings, backed by these mortgage securities, and the blind faith on conflicted credit rating agencies as arbiters of risk, the warning signals were indeed there but sadly missed by the regulators and supervisors. That their miss proved a little too costly for the world would be an understatement.

Similar things happened in the 2010 AP microfinance crisis in India. The public stewards of the system could not spot the burgeoning growth of microfinance loans in AP in 2010 and prior to that. They also could not discern the proliferation of multiple, ghost and fraudulent lending by NBFC-MFIs[1]. And the final straw on the camel's back was their inability to tackle dubious corporate governance practices at many NBFC-MFIs. Regulatory and supervisory failure was clearly a major reason for the collapse of the Indian microfinance system in 2010 in AP, and is still responsible for many of the ills associated with the financial inclusion drive thereafter.

Moving on, let us look at the U.S. $ 2 billion letters of understanding (LoU) scam of 2018, where fraudulent LoUs were used to create trade finance limits in favor of a major jeweler. While it was reportedly going on from 2011, it had been missed for almost a good solid 7 years. Here again, the captains of industry and public stewards of the system missed the issuance of not just one but (reportedly) over several hundred fraudulent LoUs at a bank branch which was hardly a stone's throw (not literally) from the headquarters of India's central bank. Clearly, this was not a mere stumble but rather

---

[1] Prior to the 2010 Indian microfinance crisis in AP, the term NBFC-MFIs refers to MFIs that were incorporated as NBFCs. The term 'NBFC-MFI' was officially introduced by the RBI after 2010.

a steep fall, and a classic case of regulatory and supervisory failure.

What can be inferred from the above? In all these cases, the public stewards of the financial sector did not police the highway, on which there were neither speed limits nor neatly painted lines—as a result, only chaos reigned supreme.

That is not all. There are more commonalities among all of these crisis situations and they afford us good lessons for the future.

In all these crisis situations, there was what I would call *widespread failures* in financial regulation and supervision, which proved devastating for financial stability. Part of the reason for this regulatory and supervisory failure was because the so-called sentries were not at their posts—primarily due to the widely accepted belief that markets often self-correct and financial institutions (banks and MFIs included) can effectively self-police themselves. Thus, the need for a steady guiding regulatory and supervisory hand at such financial institutions—which, many people argued would stifle product and process innovation—was deemed unnecessary.

Effectively speaking, consistent deregulation and increasingly greater reliance on self-regulation[2] by financial institutions, championed by many stakeholders, supported by several administrations and actively canvassed by the all-powerful financial

---

[2] Self-regulation never works in real time. It is an oxymoron.

services industry (at every possible instance everywhere) stripped away major safeguards that could have helped avoid these crisis situations and the catastrophe that followed each one. This entire self-regulation dependent approach led to serious gaps in the regulatory oversight of critical areas—all of this put billions and billions of dollars at risk across crisis situations. And what's more, governments often permitted financial service companies to pick their preferred regulators—this often became a race to the weakest examiner or supervisor.

Don't get me wrong. Despite all of this increasing reliance on self-regulation, I am not, for one second, implying that regulators and supervisors lacked the power to protect the financial system. They had enormous power in many areas and yet, when push came to shove, they chose not to use it. This is true of the U.S. subprime (2007/8) and of the Indian microfinance crisis of 2010 in AP. And where regulators lacked authority, they could have sought it. Too often, they lacked the administrative will—in an ideological environment that constrained it—as well as the fortitude to critically challenge the very set of institutions and the entire financial system they had been entrusted to oversee.

If you take a close look at the various happenings in the U.S. subprime of 2007/8 and the Indian microfinance crisis of 2010 in AP, in several instances, changes in the regulatory system occurred because the financial services industry itself played a very critical role in reducing the regulatory safeguards on financial institutions, financial markets, and financial products and services. Clearly, an industry of such enormous wealth and power could bring significant pressure on policy makers, regulators and supervisors. What was really worrisome, however, was the fact that the strength and independence of the regulators and supervisors in the financial services industry required to safeguard financial stability was slowly eroded, especially in the garb of promoting self-regulation and facilitating innovation—all with a view to enhancing inclusiveness. And a lot of this happened because of conflicts of interest at various levels and the revolving door and reverse revolving door phenomenon, whereby people from the private sector entered the regulatory domain and vice versa.

Once regulatory oversight decreased and self-regulation ruled the roost, dramatic failures of corporate governance and risk management started to occur at many systemically important financial institutions, thereby exacerbating the crisis. The commonly held regulatory view—that the desire for self-preservation inside major banks and financial institutions would hold them back from fatal risk-taking—was rendered false.

And what happened is well documented as too many of these institutions acted a little too recklessly, taking on huge risks, with very little capital, and most importantly, with too much dependence on short-term borrowings. What is really interesting to note here is that in all these crisis situations, the leverage was often hidden—in derivatives positions, in off-balance-sheet entities, and through *window dressing* of financial reports available to the investing public—in reality, no one knew the real leverage. Furthermore, the dangers of this debt were magnified because transparency was neither required nor desired. Massive, short-term borrowing, combined with obligations unseen by others in the market, heightened the chances the system could rapidly collapse.

In several instances, financial institutions and credit rating agencies started to use mathematical and other models for reliable risk prediction—replacing sound judgment laden with valuable previous experience. That was where the problem lay, because this then made risk management into mere risk justification. Overall, the above mix was certainly a huge recipe for disaster and regulators and supervisors are as much to blame as the financial institutions themselves.

In all these crisis situations, yet another common factor was the extremely poor governance of compensation, which the regulatory authorities completely missed. Designed in an environment of cheap money, severe competition, and lax regulation, these compensation systems—whether in the U.S. subprime, Indian microfinance or Indian banking crisis—too often rewarded the quick deal and short-term gains without proper consideration of medium as well as long-term risks and consequences. Often, systems encouraged the big bet—where the payoff on the upside was huge and the downside limited. This was the case up and down the line—from the corporate boardroom right down to the mortgage broker and grassroots field worker on the street.

Taken together, a combination of excessive short-term borrowing, risky investments, and lack of transparency put different facets of the financial system on a collision course with a crisis. Clearly, in effect, the failures of corporate governance, risk management and control systems and, above all, regulation and supervision can be blamed for all that went wrong on the ground, with disastrous consequences.

Two final points are in order here. In all these crisis situations, the governments, central banks, regulators and supervisors were ill-prepared, and their inconsistent response added to the uncertainty and panic in the financial system and markets. Part of the problem was that conflicts of interest were at play, as was the seamless exchange of people from the financial services industry to the regulatory domain and vice versa, because of the revolving door and reverse revolving door phenomenon.

That was not all—in all these crisis situations, there was a systemic breakdown in accountability and ethics. All of you will agree that the integrity of the financial markets and the public's trust in those markets are essential to the economic well-being of any country. The soundness, stability and the sustained prosperity of the financial system and an economy rely on the notions of fair dealing, responsibility, accountability and transparency. In any economy, we expect businesses and individuals to pursue profits—but at the same time, we also look forward to their producing need-based high quality financial services as well as conducting themselves in an ethical manner.

Unfortunately, as has been the case in past speculative booms and busts, all these crisis situations witnessed huge erosion of standards in accountability and ethics—without a doubt, the drop in standards of accountability and ethics certainly exacerbated the financial crisis. While it would be unfair to argue that the drop in ethical and accountability standards was universal and across the board, what needs to be emphasized is the fact that, often, the breaches were visible and stretched right from the grassroots level to the corporate boardroom. This had its impact not just as disastrous financial consequences but also led to a serious erosion of trust in the financial system by the public at large (which included customers, depositors, investors, end user and others), who all need to be included in a sustained manner by 2030 (as per SDG 1.3), come what may.

Before I conclude this chapter, I would like to state that the conclusions reached must be viewed in the context of human nature, as well as individual and societal responsibility. First, to pin these crisis situations entirely on mortal flaws like greed and hubris would be simplistic. It was the failure to account for human weakness that is relevant to these crisis situations.

Second, it must be emphasized that these crisis situations were the result of human mistakes, misjudgments, and misdeeds that resulted in systemic failures for which we have all paid dearly.

And special responsibility for this must lie with: a) the policy makers charged with protecting the financial system globally; b) those entrusted to run our regulatory and supervisory agencies; and c) the chief executives of banks and financial institutions whose failures drove us to these crisis situations in the first place. These individuals sought and accepted positions of significant responsibility and obligation. Yet, they did not act with responsibility and indeed, we were let down by them.

But as people and communities, we must also accept responsibility for what we permitted to occur. Collectively, but certainly not unanimously, we all embraced a system—along with its ideologies and policies—whose very actions resulted in the crisis that actually unfolded. So, we are equally responsible for the happenings. Indeed, it is in the context of the above and all that has been said in chapters 1 and 2, that the next chapter looks at the critical issue of ensuring that all men and women are financially included by 2030 and stay included thereafter. While 100% sustained financial inclusion is a laudable goal, certainly the means to achieve this enormous and far-reaching state must keep in mind what can happen when we try to turbocharge growth and push strongly towards the above goal. The larger point being made here is that whatever we do has to be done responsibly and without creating another crisis.

Chapter 3

Financial Inclusion, Towards Accountable Progress

Poverty, and especially rising economic inequality, are the most fundamental problems that we face globally. As President Barack Obama is reported to have said in his departing speech at the United Nations in 2016, "A world where 1% of humanity has the same wealth as the remaining 99% of people, can never be stable."[1] Indeed, four years after the world economic forum first identified rising economic inequality as the most fundamental problem, very little has happened on the ground. Financial inclusion can play a tremendous role in helping to fight not only economic inequality but also poverty. And indeed

---

[1] See 'Read Barack Obama's Final Speech to the United Nations as President', September 20, 2016, *Time.com,* Katie Reilly, http://time.com/4501910/president-obama-united-nations-speech-transcript/

that is why 100% financial inclusion by 2030 is stated as sub-goal 1.3 under the United Nation's Sustainable Development Goals (UN SDGs).

However, if financial inclusion is to play a meaningful role in tackling poverty and rising economic inequality in real time, financial inclusion—as a process and paradigm—must change, and change fundamentally. In short, financial inclusion must always strive to enhance the bargaining, staying and negotiating power of small producers, farmers, low-income people, micro, small and medium enterprises (MSMEs) and other excluded people in various supply chains and thereby enable them to stay included always. Sustained financial inclusion is the key and the financial inclusion paradigm must strive to ensure that the various financial inclusion services, products, processes, financial institutions, delivery channels, etc., are so structured that they allow excluded—mutually exclusive—people, once included, to stay included always.

Furthermore, this paradigm shift requires fundamental changes to the financial inclusion paradigm and two aspects are important here. One is the definition of financial inclusion in a clear, comprehensive manner that is universally acceptable in a global sense and yet adaptable to different strategic contexts. Despite the billions and billions of dollars invested in financial inclusion, we still do not even have that. Only when we have a universally accepted definition of financial inclusion, can measuring it become possible in real time. The second and more important aspect is the measurement of financial inclusion anytime, anywhere in terms of the actual number of mutually exclusive individuals having access to financial inclusion services—it needs to be emphasized that I am talking of population data here and not survey-based data, which are absolutely useless and meaningless as financial inclusion is a highly individual specific dynamic construct wherein people get included, excluded, and re-included all the time. The above is very important because while there has been a lot of talk about financial inclusion, there is very little known about how to measure financial inclusion. To the best of my knowledge, I am not aware of any robust measures of financial inclusion that have been used by financial service regulators, finance ministries and/or central banks worldwide.

Realistically speaking, if we are to make serious progress towards eradicating or mitigating poverty as per the sustainable development goals, then it is imperative that we have 100% sustained financial inclusion. This is the essence of UN SDG 1, of which UN SDG 1.3 (100% financial inclusion) is a part. This in turn requires us to do two things: a) define financial inclusion in a comprehensive manner so that it is accepted universally; and b) develop truly reliable and valid measures of financial inclusion. Only then can we say where we are—in a true and objective sense—with regard to financial inclusion as of today, and only if we know this can we meaningfully move towards 100% (sustained) financial inclusion by 2030.[2] And unless we know where we are today with regard to financial inclusion, we will not be able to decide on strategies that will take us to where we want to be in the future. Furthermore, without such reliable and valid measures, we will not be able to know if we have really reached our destination with regard to financial inclusion.

For a long time, I have been looking for reliable and valid data on how many (mutually exclusive) people are financially included at any given point in time across the globe. The question that I pose is whether we can state the number of mutually exclusive people included financially as at this instance in the world by continent? Do we at least have this data disaggregated by country? Forget country level data. Can we provide these financial inclusion statistics by state or district (province) within a country? Or at least can we provide this data for our own community or neighbourhood? The answer is sadly 'no'. We cannot provide any of this and that is the reality, unfortunately. And undoubtedly, this makes the task of measuring progress towards SDG 1.3 (100% financial inclusion) a very difficult one as we neither have reliable and valid measures of the

---

[2] This is indeed a very critical point to note and all stakeholders involved in the financial inclusion industry should take immediate and necessary steps to not only define financial inclusion comprehensively but, more importantly, also use the same to build robust, reliable and valid measures of financial inclusion—otherwise we simply will be talking in thin air and cannot make accountable progress towards UN SDG 1.3 (i.e., 100% [sustained] financial inclusion) which is to be achieved by 2030 in order to help realize SDG 1 (a world free of poverty by 2030).

dynamic financial inclusion construct nor the required data in terms of the actual number of mutually exclusive people who are financially included at any instant—by continent, country, state, region, locality and/or neighbourhood.

I have also been looking for hard numbers on how many mutually exclusive people were financially included in a given country in a specific year. That's not all. I was also trying to determine, across countries, the number of mutually exclusive people who had been financially included but were forced to exit the financial system for some reason or another. However, none of this is available.

The truth is that, despite living in a data driven world, often we are unable to get the data we want. I was in fact talking to a few friends at different central banks and associated ministries of finance in countries in Asia, Africa, North America, Caribbean and Latin America. I asked them for basic data on financial inclusion. They were unable to tell me the actual number of mutually exclusive individuals who were financially included at any point in time in their country. Not just that. They were also unable to tell me the actual number of mutually exclusive individuals who had been financially included in the most recent or preceding financial year. And of course, they had no idea whatsoever about the actual number of mutually exclusive individuals who had been forced to exit the financial system for one reason or another during the most recent or preceding financial year.

I was amazed and I told them that unless the importance of having such up-to-date, reliable, valid and transparent data on financial inclusion is emphasized by all of them (as key stakeholders), why would the financial inclusion industry even think of such data? So the key action point going forward for central banks and ministries of finance (in various governments) is that they must start to devise an enabling policy framework that outlines practical strategies for collecting, collating, storing and disseminating this crucial financial inclusion data, so that accountable progress towards SDG 1.3 (100% financial inclusion) can be easily tracked. With the kind of technology we have today, it should be easily possible.

Why is it important to have this data?

There are three good reasons for us to have this data and each of them, которые are equally essential, are given below.

One, there is no one single accepted universal definition of financial inclusion. When is a person financially included[3]? When is a person financially excluded? Is financial inclusion the mere accessing of a financial service? Or is it the accessing of a financial service regularly or continuously? Two, financial inclusion by itself is a dynamic construct. Someone who is included today need not be included tomorrow. In other words, financial inclusion is a

---

[3] We really need to specify what financial inclusion really means—both in a general sense (in terms of the scope of financial inclusion) and also specifically with regard to various financial services!

cycle that repeats itself, much as history does. Three, we have no means of ensuring that the total number—of financially included people—that we arrive at is a mutually exclusive number, as in many countries of this world there exists no unique identifier. And without a mutually exclusive number (regarding people financially included at any instance), we would not have an accurate figure with regard to financial inclusion in terms of where we are today. Indeed, I fail to understand how one can build towards a vision for financial inclusion[4] without reliable, valid and transparent data—one that is based on unique identifiers—on where we are today.

Only if we know 'where we are today' in terms of financial inclusion, can we decide on a strategy that will take us from 'where we are' to 'where we want to be'. Clearly, if we don't know 'where we are today', we cannot decide on how to get to 'where we want to be tomorrow'. This is similar to a journey where we do not know our point of departure for travelling. That being the case, how can we decide on a meaningful strategy to reach a specific known destination? Without a doubt, with billions of dollars being spent on financial inclusion annually, it's about time we get more strategic and precise with regard to financial inclusion and track its progress in an accountable and transparent manner.

---

[4] The vision is UN SDG 1.3 which calls for 100% financial inclusion by 2030.

Getting back to the definitional aspects, what constitutes financial inclusion[5]? Is it the opening of a bank account, despite the same lying dormant? Is it the receipt of multiple (concurrent) loans which render the recipient a defaulter, as in undivided Andhra Pradesh 2010? Is the mere downloading of bank or wallet mobile applications (for example, like the Bharat Interface for Money [BHIM] or Paytm in India or M-Pesa in Kenya) financial inclusion, despite irregular or no usage? Is it the purchase of health insurance, where clients have to wait endlessly for the payout? That is not all! Are financially included clients regularly tracked to see if they remain active and included users thereafter? For example, if a client exits the formal financial system after having used a financial service for a specified period of time, how does the current inclusion paradigm[6] treat this client? Is she/he counted as an included or excluded client?

And most importantly, with a huge amount of resources being used by the financial inclusion sector,[7] is there not a duty and responsibility to track and accurately report on it? Why are ministries of

---

[5] I guess, if one thinks it through carefully, then financial inclusion may be described as the 'process' of continuously accessing a financial service and/or a set of related/unrelated financial services. Financial inclusion may thus be defined as a 'process' by which individuals build a normal, regular and consistent relationship with a formal, semi-formal financial or new age (digital financial) institution, by accessing their products or services. Regular and consistent may be interpreted in common parlance as per prevailing laws.

[6] Unfortunately, currently the financial inclusion paradigm makes no effort whatsoever to track already included clients who may get excluded in the normal course of life.

[7] On a global basis, billions and billions of U.S. dollars are invested and/or spent on financial inclusion, to say the least.

finance, central banks and other regulators (in various countries) globally not measuring the dynamic construct of financial inclusion and tracking it continuously? These stakeholders, who are extremely good at collating and putting out data, have somehow not seen the importance of the above data, which I believe is crucial for enhancing financial inclusion on a worldwide basis. There is yet another issue here. With billions and billions of dollars going into what we call financial inclusion globally and with the set sub-goal of 100% financial inclusion by 2030 (as per SDG 1.3), why have the concerned stakeholders—in the public and private sector as well as governments and international agencies—not attempted to create reliable and valid measures that will help (us) track accountable progress towards SDG 1.3?

While some people may argue that sample surveys—to measure the level of financial inclusion—exist, surveys,[8] unfortunately, cannot help track progress towards SDG 1.3 because financial inclusion is a highly individual specific dynamic construct, where people can get included and excluded repeatedly because of a dynamically changing environment.

What we need are reliable and valid measures that will help us track the number of mutually exclusive individuals financially included at anytime, anywhere. With the kind of resources we have it is possible and, more importantly, it can be achieved in a very cost

---

[8] The aspects of using sample surveys to measure the level of financial inclusion is very erroneous and is discussed at appropriate places throughout the book. Refer to these discussions.

effective manner. The inclusive finance industry and its torch bearers must wake up to this reality that having reliable and valid measures—that will help us track the number of mutually exclusive individuals financially included at anytime, anywhere—is critical today and for going forward.

Specifically, we need to know how many mutually exclusive individuals are financially included at any given moment. We would also need to know with regard to any financial year: a) how many mutually exclusive individuals were financially included at the beginning of the concerned financial year?; b) how many mutually exclusive individuals were financially included during the concerned financial year?; c) how many mutually exclusive individuals—who were financially included at the beginning of the concerned financial year—exited the financial system during the same year and the reasons for doing so?; and d) how many mutually exclusive individuals were still financially included as at the end of the concerned financial year?

We need answers to these questions, year on year, if indeed we are serious about achieving SDG 1.3 and tracking progress towards it in a reliable and valid manner in real time. This is to set the record straight.

Indeed, if the UN SDG goal 1 target is to be met by 2030, we urgently need to have comprehensive measures of the dynamic construct of financial inclusion, where people get included and excluded financially in a cycle. Only then can we tailor our strategies accordingly and facilitate our efforts so as to meet this goal.

And for all of this, the key task ahead is to build a country-by-country (decentralized) data repository on the following:
- Number of mutually exclusive individuals financially included at the beginning of each financial year, which we can call as $A_{(year)}$;
- Number of mutually exclusive individuals who are financially included during each financial year, which we can call as $B_{(year)}$; and
- Number of mutually exclusive (financially included) individuals who exited the financial system during each financial year, which we can call as $C_{(year)}$.

This will help us get to the year-end position, which represents the number of mutually exclusive individuals financially included at end of each financial year, which we can call as $D_{(year)}$.

Now, $D_{(year)} = A_{(year)} + B_{(year)} - C_{(year)}$. **Box 3.1** provides an illustrative example of the above, using the case of life insurance.

> **Box 3.1: How to Measure Financial Inclusion:
> The Case of Life Insurance!**
>
> We first need the number of mutually exclusive (unique ID associated) individuals holding active life insurance policies at the beginning of the financial year. Active is defined in common parlance as the respective insurance act(s). This is financial inclusion with regard to life insurance as at the beginning of the year and let us call it $A_{(year)}$.
>
> Then we need the number of mutually exclusive individuals who purchased life insurance policies during the concerned financial year. This is financial inclusion that occurred during the year and let us call it $B_{(year)}$.
>
> Thereafter, we need to know the number of mutually exclusive individuals—who either held active policies at the beginning of the financial year or purchased policies during the financial year—whose policy status changed from active to inactive (or lapsed) during the year. This is financial exclusion during the year and let us call this $C_{(year)}$.
>
> Furthermore, we need to know the number of mutually exclusive individuals whose policies were paid out during the year. This can be called $D_{(year)}$. I would put these people under the realm of financially included as they had neither defaulted nor dropped out—rather, they availed the financial service to its complete logical end.
>
> We also need the number of inactive policy holders at the financial year beginning whose policies became active during the year—let us call this $E_{(year)}$.
>
> Then we can calculate the number of mutually exclusive individuals holding active life insurance policies at the end of the financial year. Active is defined in common parlance as per respective laws. This is the year-end financial inclusion and let us call this $F_{(year)}$.
>
> $$F_{(year)} = A_{(year)} + B_{(year)} - C_{(year)} - D_{(year)} + E_{(year)}$$

This is just one example and, like this, it should be possible to obtain the above data across other financial inclusion services and track it across the years, and it will help us determine whether our financial products, processes and strategies are appropriate. We will also get to know causative factors for financial exclusion and thereby help tailor our products, processes, delivery channels, etc., accordingly. When we have this data across the globe for all kinds of financial services coming under the ambit of financial inclusion, disaggregated by continent, country, region, gender, age, ethnicity etc, we should be able to meaningfully track progress towards 100% (sustained) financial inclusion as per SDG 1.3—a goal that we have all committed to achieving.

For the above, the respective ministries of finance (along with various financial services regulators) in every country must first define financial inclusion precisely[9] and start the journey[10] for immediately tracking and ensuring 100% (sustained) financial inclusion by 2030.

---

[9] For example, I have seen the websites and documents of over 50 Central banks and they do not have a precise definition of financial inclusion.

[10] This, in turn, calls for availability of precise definitions of financial inclusion services, active financial inclusion clients and financial inclusion service providers—all of these need to be evolved and used for tracking and ensuring progress towards SDG 1.3.

In tangible terms, what needs to be done for all the above to be achieved?

Ministries of finance, central banks and other financial sector regulators (in the respective countries) need to first include the word financial inclusion in their preamble of their bare acts.[11]

Second, they must also specify financial inclusion as a core area of their interest.

Third, the annual reports of all regulators should have an entire chapter devoted to financial inclusion, which must, among other things, spell out the number of mutually exclusive financially included people at the beginning of the financial year, the number of mutually exclusive people who were financially included during the financial year, the number of mutually exclusive people who were financially included at the beginning of the year but who exited the financial system during the year for some reason or the other and the year-end figure of the number of mutually exclusive financially included people.

Box 3.2 outlines the above mathematically.

---

[11] Financial inclusion is fundamental to any country and every economy and therefore has to become an integral part of every financial service regulator's mandate and functions. The world of yesterday is not the same as that of today and the world of tomorrow will not be the same as that of today. Therefore, the mandate and functions of financial service regulators will also have to undergo changes to reflect the current reality. And much of the same applies to the respective ministries of finance as well.

> **Box 3.2: Annual Reports of Financial Service Regulators and Chapter on Financial Inclusion**
>
> What data should central banks and other financial service regulators have with regard to financial inclusion in their annual reports, so as to ensure accountable progress with regard to financial inclusion? I see the following as the most critical data that they should include in their annual reports, preferably through an exclusive chapter:
>
> A) The number of mutually exclusive individuals who were financially included at the beginning of the financial year;
> B) The number of mutually exclusive individuals who were financially included during the financial year;
> C) The number of mutually exclusive individuals who, for some reason or other, were forced to exit the financial system and thereby financially excluded during the financial year; and
> D) The number of mutually exclusive individuals who were financially included at the end of the year.
>
> In other words, $D = A + B - C$. Kindly note the emphasis on <u>mutually exclusive</u> individuals. That is critical, and it requires the use of a unique identifier (unique ID associated with a unique individual)—like Aadhaar is used in India—for know your customer (KYC) compliance. This, in effect, would mean every transaction is associated with a unique ID and unique person. If ministries of finance (in the respective countries), central banks and other financial service regulators were to do the above, then we are likely to have accountable progress towards financial inclusion and also evaluate the extent to which we are progressing towards the sustainable development goal 1.3, which calls for 100% (sustained) financial inclusion by 2030.

Ministries of finance (in the respective countries), central banks and other regulators also need to create a regulator sponsored decentralized data repository—based on the distributed ledger technology

(DLT[12])—which contains data of all transactions within the ambit of financial inclusion. And each and every transaction in this data repository will be associated with a unique ID which, in turn, will be associated with a mutually exclusive (unique) individual. As noted earlier, it goes without saying that the unique ID must be made mandatory for KYC compliance by all the financial service regulators and special provisions will have to be made by them to ensure their safety and prevent misuse of the unique ID.[13]

Only this will give us credible, reliable and valid data on financial inclusion and allow us to track accountable progress with regard to the billions of dollars being used up by financial inclusion. Also, this will enable us to know how many mutually exclusive individuals are included at a point in time, how many financially excluded mutually exclusive individuals entered the financial system in any given financial year, how many financially included mutually exclusive individuals exited the financial system in any given financial year, and so on. All of this

---

[12] A distributed ledger is fundamentally a database of (financial, legal, physical or electronic) assets that can be shared across a network of multiple sites, geographies or institutions. The most wonderful aspect is that all participants within the network have their own identical copy of the ledger. And any changes to the ledger are reflected in all copies—at the earliest within seconds and at the latest within minutes. The security and accuracy of the various assets in the ledger are maintained cryptographically through the use of 'keys' and signatures—this is to control who can perform what actions within the shared ledger. Entries can also be updated by one, some or all of the participants, according to rules agreed by the network, which often has multi-stakeholder governance.

[13] The unique ID will be stored on a permissioned blockchain.

information will thus help us bring about on-course corrections with regard to ensuring sustained financial inclusion and thereby help achieve SDG 1.3 which is 100% sustained financial inclusion by 2030.

To re-emphasize, it is mandatory that we define financial inclusion in a comprehensive and measurable manner.[14]

This would entail identifying the products/services that are part of financial inclusion; the processes through which these services are delivered; the institutions, including new age ones, who deliver these services; the places from where these services are delivered; and so on.

---

[14] *Some examples of products and services (not-exhaustive)*: 1) Having and using a savings/current account regularly; 2) Having a functional recurring/fixed deposit; 3) Servicing any form of debt in a regular and consistent manner; 4) Accessing pension funds, insurance, risk management, mutual funds/investment, payment/remittance services etc and maintaining a normal functional relationship with concerned institutions. Normal defined in common parlance and universally accepted standards; 5) Regular and normal use of prepaid instruments like digital (mobile) wallets; and 6) Accessing and utilizing capital market and other financial services as and when required. I think ministries of finance along with financial service regulators in the respective countries must start to put out precise definitions of financial inclusion—one that is globally acceptable yet adaptive to the local country context. Only then will we be able to really take stock of 'where we are today' and measure progress towards 'where we want to be tomorrow'. Further, outreach and access data will be reliable and valid only then, bereft of the usual double and triple counting that we normally see.

And unless we know what services constitute financial inclusion, the processes by which they are delivered or produced, the institutions delivering them, the places from which these services are delivered, we cannot even think of reliable, valid, up-to-date, transparent and measurable data on financial inclusion, which is so vital for accountable progress and especially to achieve SDG 1.3.

Now, all of the above require a policy framework at the country level and this framework must address several issues.

First, the framework must provide a precise definition of what constitutes financial inclusion. The definition must specify the range of financial services that come under financial inclusion and the stakeholders and financial institutions involved. The definition must be conceptually valid and capable of operationalization in real terms. In other words, it cannot be abstract.

Second, the framework must provide for the use of a unique identifier (unique ID) with regard to all kinds of financial inclusion services on all occasions so that anywhere, anytime measurement of financial inclusion is possible in terms of mutually exclusive individuals. This entails specifying rules and procedures with regard to the same.

Third, the framework must also provide the overarching conceptual underpinnings and implementation framework with regard to the ongoing collection, utilization and analysis of comprehensive, up-to-date, reliable and valid data with regard to financial inclusion in terms of mutually exclusive individuals at anytime, anywhere.

Fourth, the framework must also use the above and outline regulatory and supervisory arrangements with regard to financial inclusion, especially using RegTech[15] and other state of the art techniques.

Without a doubt, we cannot be in the dark with regard to financial inclusion anymore and rely on inappropriate sample surveys that primarily feed us incomplete and inaccurate information on financial inclusion.

And based on the above policy framework, we need clear-cut actionable policy guidelines on financial inclusion from ministries of finance (in consultation with central banks and other financial service regulators) in every country.

---

[15] RegTech is broadly defined as the use and deployment of technology for regulation and supervision by regulators and supervisors. Here, we are talking of the financial services sector but the same can apply to other sectors as well. RegTech can also be used by regulators in the fields of telecommunications, electricity, education, healthcare and so on. See the chapter on RegTech for a more detailed perspective on the use of RegTech and its applications.

And in my opinion, ministries of finance are the real guardians of financial inclusion for several reasons: a) They are the custodians of the economy and therefore have the mandate to ensure that each and every person in their country has easy, timely, convenient and affordable access to a wide range of need-based financial services from the available formal/semi-formal financial institutions; b) By virtue of their role in the economy, ministries of finance are also responsible for how an economy performs and, from that perspective, the greater the financial inclusion, the larger the economy and, perhaps, the better its performance; and c) They are neutral, compared to other stakeholders who drive financial inclusion and they typically have no products and services to sell.

They therefore have no vested interest in pushing the agenda of financial inclusion other than the larger public good.

For these and other reasons, ministries of finance must now take charge of financial inclusion and create a suitable policy framework that defines it precisely, mandate use of a unique identifier (see **Box 3.3** below) for financial inclusion, ensure availability of comprehensive, reliable, valid, up-to-date and transparent data on financial inclusion and thereby help track accountable progress towards financial inclusion.

> **Box 3.3: The Need for a Unique Identifier**
>
> One of the most critical ingredients for having up-to-date, reliable, valid and transparent data on financial inclusion is the presence and use of a unique identifier (like Aadhaar[16] in India). A unique identifier will ensure that the data associated with each unique ID is reliable and valid because each unique ID is associated with a unique individual only. Therefore, any data repository that uses the unique ID as its fulcrum will naturally ensure that only data of mutually exclusive individuals are used—among other things, this eliminates the distortion and noise associated with typical financial inclusion data such as double or triple counting of outreach/access data, snapshot perspective and so on. Therefore, it is very important for ministries of finance and all financial service regulators in the respective countries to integrate a unique identifier (unique ID) into the financial inclusion policy framework in an official sense. This unique identifier will then have to be made mandatory by central banks and other financial services regulators for KYC compliance by financial institutions including banks, MFIs, insurance companies, pension funds and others—this will ensure that every financial transaction is associated with a unique ID and thereby with a unique person/individual.
>
> This is the first and most crucial step that we have to take towards ensuring up-to-date, reliable, valid and transparent data with regard to financial inclusion. Without doubt, data on mutually exclusive individuals based on a unique identifier will give us a true picture of financial inclusion on the ground and help us towards enhancing the same in a meaningful and sustainable manner. Of course, it will also help in tracking accountable progress towards SDG 1.3. And it goes without saying that care would have to be taken to ensure the safety, privacy and security of all the data that is associated with each unique ID.

---

[16] See 'Aadhaar', *Wikipedia,* https://en.wikipedia.org/wiki/Aadhaar and 'Unique ID', *UIDAI,* https://uidai.gov.in/

To summarize, to me, one of the biggest problems that we face in financial inclusion is how to track (in a reliable and valid manner) the progress towards 100% financial inclusion by 2030 (SDG 1.3). This sub-goal is especially important in achieving sustainable development goal (SDG) 1. Reliability and validity of measures in tracking progress towards 100% financial inclusion are therefore very, very necessary.

SDG goal 1 talks about a world without poverty (in all its forms) everywhere! Goal 1 targets include: "By 2030, ensure that *all men and women*, in particular the poor and the vulnerable, have equal rights to economic resources, as well as access to ...financial services, including microfinance."[17]

If the goal 1 target is to be met by 2030, then its sub-goals will have to be met and the same goes for SDG 1.3, which calls for 100% (sustained) financial inclusion (i.e., all men and women having access to financial services, including microfinance), we urgently need to have a comprehensive definition of financial inclusion along with reliable and valid measures of the dynamic construct of financial inclusion, where people get included and excluded financially in a cycle.

Only then can we tailor our financial inclusion strategies accordingly and achieve SDGs 1 and 1.3 by years 2030 and thereby create a world free of poverty where billions of individuals—irrespective of gender,

---

[17] See 'Goal 1: End poverty in all its forms everywhere', https://www.un.org/sustainabledevelopment/poverty/

ethnicity, class, caste, age, religion, education etc—are able to easily (and in a sustained manner) access need-based, quality and affordable financial services[18] and thereby realize their dreams.

And before I sign off, one point is in order here. While defining financial inclusion is critical, we also need to understand the salient issues with regard to this dynamic construct. That is indeed the subject of the next chapter.

---

[18] I am talking of delivery of various financial services at scale by a range of institutions—new age as well as eclectic—in a sustainable manner.

Chapter 4

Financial Inclusion, Salient Issues

The earlier chapter looked at the lack of data with regard to financial inclusion and argued for the collecting, collating, analyzing and disseminating of the same to track accountable progress towards financial inclusion and, in particular, SDG 1.3. In this somewhat related chapter, I want to emphasize a few critical points with regard to financial inclusion so that we can move towards a new paradigm of financial inclusion—which will not only help address extant problems on the ground but also allow us to conduct our long journey towards SDG 1.3—i.e., 100% (sustained) financial inclusion by 2030—in a seamless, accountable and transparent manner.

First is the fact that financial inclusion is a dynamic construct. It is not a one-time affair. People who get financially included don't stay that way for ever. Some exit the financial system, and few find their way back. Others get included again. In other words, what it means is that there is a cycle of financial inclusion, financial exclusion, financial re-inclusion and so on. Financial inclusion is thus like a game of musical chairs and I can say this based on my near 30-year experience of working globally in over 26 countries and about 610 of India's 640 districts. What this effectively means is that people are not permanently included. Rather, people enter the financial system and thereafter also exit the financial system, perhaps only to be re-included again[1] and that's a crucial fact that we need to keep in mind while designing products, services, processes, delivery channels and financial institutions, while measuring and tracking financial inclusion.

Two issues are important here: a) One, we need to recognize the dynamic nature of financial inclusion

---

[1] Agricultural finance is a classic example of financially included people going through a repeated cycle of inclusion and exclusion. In many agrarian economies, ensuring that financially included people stay included for the rest of their active lives (at the least), is necessary for achieving SDG 1.3 by 2030. This whole notion of financial inclusion being a static phenomenon is rather peculiar. Inclusion is a dynamic activity and people get included and excluded, time and again. Many of the families that were (financially) included in the integrated rural development programme (IRDP) in India were subsequently excluded. Likewise, some farmers who were included in the mainstream financial system (before the major agriculture debt waiver that happened in 2008/2009 in India) have perhaps now been excluded. Similarly, perhaps many of the clients who did not repay in the aftermath of the 2010 Andhra Pradesh microfinance crisis in India, have now become official 'defaulters'—as the credit bureaus have come to classify them—and thereby are (re) excluded again!

and develop appropriate measures that capture this dynamism in the construct of financial inclusion. It is the critical need of the hour today.

And unless we have these measures that can capture the dynamic nature of financial inclusion, the progress made in financial inclusion will remain as ambiguous as it has been during the period 2005-2018. It is about time that the global financial inclusion industry adopted appropriate financial inclusion yardsticks and measures for tracking the dynamic nature of financial inclusion, thereby facilitating greater accountability and enhanced transparency in real time; and

b) Two, a key learning point for me here has been the fact that it is very important to understand how people who were once financially included ultimately got excluded. Such an analysis should help us better understand systemic factors and causes that result in the exclusion of financially included people. Therefore, what needs to be critically looked at is why clients were forced to leave the financial system and/or are pushed out of it, where they go when this happens, and how they can be meaningfully re-included. These are not exhaustive questions by any means but rather simple starter issues that should bother well-meaning financial inclusion strategists immensely—and only then can we make the walk back into the first mile of the financial system a pleasant and lasting experience. Let us make no mistake about that! The above analysis is equivalent to the analysis of dropouts that has traditionally been carried out in the financial services sector. Without a doubt, such an analysis will go a long way towards understanding causative factors with regard to financial inclusion and exclusion. That in itself would prove to be a great contribution to the practice of financial inclusion globally, as it will help us develop better financial inclusion products, processes, institutions, delivery channels and so on. Armed with this knowledge, we can hopefully create products, institutions and processes—i.e., an entire financial inclusion ecosystem—that facilitate financially included people to stay included always. This is most crucial.

Second, we have always talked of the sustainability of institutions and so on. That is great and necessary. But what about, for a change, also focusing on making the client and/or end user of the financial inclusion product or service sustainable? Wealth creation is critical for this, which in turn requires sustained financial inclusion—something that will happen, if and only if, the entire financial ecosystem, apart from being sustainable, looks at enhancing the bargaining, staying and negotiating power of the client (or end user) and also reducing their vulnerabilities. And all of the above work in reinforcing each other towards building an inclusive ecosystem that ensures sustained financial inclusion in the long run, whereby people once included stay included for perpetuity. And that alone can ensure the goal of 100% anywhere, anytime sustained financial inclusion—an aspect critical for achieving SDG 1.3.

Third, let us ask ourselves the question as to why knowing the exact number of (mutually exclusive) financially included people at any instance worldwide is so important. There are three critical reasons for this. One, financial inclusion is a necessary condition for not only lifting people out of poverty but also for addressing inequality, that has become the bane of societies worldwide. Two, going by the above, financial inclusion is tantamount to a fundamental right for people to live a life of dignity and this applies to all countries across the world. Three, we, as countries and their people, have collectively formulated what is commonly referred to as The United Nation's sustainable development goals (SDGs), wherein we have committed to eradicate poverty by the year 2030—UN SDG goal number one. In fact, goal number one[2] has 100% (sustained) financial inclusion by 2030 as its sub-goal (SDG 1.3) and to track progress towards this in a transparent and accountable manner, we need to know the actual number of (mutually exclusive) financially included people at any instant worldwide.

Fourth, what does 100% financial inclusion by 2030 mean? Every person,[3] irrespective of gender, religion, class, caste, creed or color, continues to have regular

---

[2] What does UN SDG Goal 1 say? It argues for ending poverty in all its forms everywhere. Goal 1 also argues that "by 2030, ensure that all men and women, in particular the poor and the vulnerable, have equal rights to economic resources, as well as access to financial services, including microfinance." Thus, 100% (sustained) financial inclusion by 2030 is a sub-goal to be achieved.

[3] Person is generally supposed to mean adult, although adults can borrow for the health and/or educational needs of their minor children.

and on-going opportunities to access a wide range of need-based, affordable, high quality financial services[4] delivered in a transparent and customer centric manner by financial institutions,[5] and they are able to use the same (without disruption) for perpetuity. In fact, SDG 1.3 is a crucial concept, because implied in its definition is the concept of sustained financial inclusion whereby people once included, stay included for perpetuity. That is the correct interpretation of SDG 1.3, as our goal is 100% (sustained) financial inclusion by 2030.

For this, knowing the number of people financially included at any instance is critical. Yet, we have nothing in our kitty that can provide this crucial information, despite all the money, resources, big data analytics and the like that we possess. Indeed, if you put a number on the total money spent on enhancing financial inclusion globally, it would run into billions and billions of dollars. And despite this, we cannot provide a clear and accurate picture on the level of financial inclusion worldwide at any instance—something which is crucial for understanding our real and transparent progress towards sustained financial inclusion, as per SDG 1.3.

---

[4] The range of financial services should ideally include a wide spectrum comprising of savings, credit, risk management (i.e., insurance and pensions), investment, digital finance and other services as appropriate.
[5] This should ideally include formal/semi-formal institutions as well as registered moneylenders.

That is simply not acceptable because it leaves us with a lot of unanswered questions. For one, how are we going to meaningfully track our progress towards SDG 1.3 that argues for 100% (sustained) financial inclusion by 2030? Likewise, unless we know which of the people whom we considered as included at a specific instance, exited the financial system (subsequently during a period) and for what reason, how will we be able to enhance the quality of financial inclusion services and prevent dropouts? This is, again, something that is so crucial for achieving 100% (sustained) financial inclusion by 2030.

Fifth, as mentioned earlier, sample surveys like the global Findex survey[6] are of no real use when it comes to measuring a dynamic construct like financial inclusion in a reliable and valid manner. Sample surveys offer just a snapshot of a dynamic construct like financial inclusion, based on (so-called) representational data. They are not at all suitable for measuring progress towards 100% sustained financial inclusion as per SDG 1.3. This is because financial inclusion is dynamic in nature and the financially excluded can be included but there is nothing to prevent them from being excluded again. History is replete with examples of this musical chair arrangement that see people entering and exiting the financial system in a jiffy.

---

[6] As noted in this book, the global Findex survey and other such efforts cannot and will not help us track progress towards 100% financial inclusion as mandated by SDG 1.3.

Let us remember that financial inclusion is quite unlike the literacy continuum where, for example, a person once included will remain forever within it. An illiterate individual can become literate but once literate, she/he cannot ever go back to being illiterate as long as the parameters remain a constant. In other words, if the definition of literacy remains the same, the literate will continue to remain literate. Alternatively, a financially included person can exit the continuum at any point and go back to being financially excluded, even while the parameters for judging financial inclusion remain the same. Thus, comprehensive *real time population data on mutually exclusive individuals* worldwide is necessary for measuring progress towards SDG 1.3. Therefore, sample surveys are of no real use for tracking progress towards financial inclusion, especially in relation to SDG 1.3.

So, if we are really serious about achieving SDG sub-goal (1.3) of 100% sustained financial inclusion by 2030, creating reliable, valid and transparent measures/data on the same is crucial. When Kermal Darvis, former United Nations Development Programme (UNDP) administrator, released my India country paper[7] for UNDP on financial inclusion in 2008, I stressed the urgent need for such measures/data on financial inclusion. I had hoped that all the stakeholders would take up this matter with the utmost urgency, but almost a decade has gone by with no real reliable/valid measures in sight.

---

[7] See appendix 1.

Sixth, without proper baseline data, quoting facts and figures on financial inclusion is meaningless, as then we would not be able to attribute whether financial inclusion occurred because of something we did consciously or if it was simply an accidental happening and/or act of god. *When we cannot say how many people are financially included at any given instance by gender, race, class, caste, age, etc., across countries and continents, how can we track progress meaningfully?*

Having an internally consistent definition of financial inclusion is therefore very critical. And generating baseline data based on the same is even more important. Together, these can form the basis for our opinions and judgments, which in turn can shape a policy and its subsequent implementation appropriately. Here, the priority task would be to know how many mutually exclusive individuals are financially included at any given instance. And when we say financially included, we need to be able to disaggregate this figure in terms of services/products accessed by these *mutually exclusive individuals* through different channels (and their institutions) and *across various regions/states* in a country across countries. If this basic (baseline) data becomes available, then we can analyze the data to get better analytics about the rural-urban divide, demographics and so on.

Seventh, my grassroots journey in about 610 districts of India and over 26 countries during the last 30 years has clearly shown me that we lack transparent and accurate outreach data with regard to banks,

MFIs[8] and their clients as well. There is much overlap in clients across banks and MFIs and, especially, across models in many countries. All of these lead to significant exaggeration in outreach data. Further, data on know your customer (KYC) norms, lending to agriculture, insurance services and pensions also have their problems and thereby contribute to outreach exaggeration.

Thus, given that there is so much double and triple counting and exaggeration in the outreach data, it is imperative that we know the real outreach in terms of *mutually exclusive individuals first*. I hope that the ministries of finance in the respective countries will set in motion appropriate processes, like incorporation of a unique identifier (unique ID), so that transparent data which can lend itself to objective field verification is publicly available. We need to know how many mutually exclusive individuals have been reached under various financial inclusion efforts—as this would also entail significant coordination with other regulators, as well as the central bank. Again, ministries of finance in the respective countries would need to ensure appropriate coordination.

---

[8] See appendix 1.

Eighth, typically speaking, the scope of financial inclusion involves the following related services (not exhaustive):

1. Access to savings and current accounts
2. Access to fixed and recurring deposits
3. Access to transaction banking, including through the internet and mobile[9]
4. Access to credit facilities including FinTech loans[10]
5. Access to risk management services[11]
6. Access to other services[12]
7. Digital services[13]

---

[9] This would include use of cheques, demand drafts and other such instruments; receiving of social security payments through bank accounts; transfer of money through various remittance services; use of debit cards, ATMs and credit cards; payments through prepaid instruments like wallets.

[10] a) Typical loans for agriculture and allied areas etc; b) Post-harvest, post production loans; c) Loans for marketing of agricultural and other produce etc; d) Traditional term loans and working capital limits; e) Traditional MSME loans; f) Traditional MFI/NBFI loans; g) Loans from specialized credit and other cooperatives; h) Traditional MSME loans backed by credit guarantee from Governments; i) Housing/mortgage loans; j) Various kinds of overdraft facilities; and k) FinTech loans.

[11] a) Life insurance; b) Health insurance; c) Asset insurance; d) Crop and weather insurance; e) Livestock insurance; f) Other such products such as credit insurance; and g) Micro-pensions etc.,

[12] a) deposit insurance; b) business facilitators (BF) and business correspondents (BC); c) financial literacy services and credit counseling centers; d) consumer protection, grievance redressal, ombudsman and legal aid services; e) credit bureau; and f) other services

[13] A range of digital finance services including remittances, transfers and payments, credit, savings, insurance and other services through various kinds of digital instruments and wallets.

And among the above,[14] financial inclusion is presently characterized by:

- Preoccupation with the opening of savings bank accounts or digital accounts
- Large focus on consumption credit and small production loans[15]
- Low outreach with regard to vulnerable groups in agriculture
- Lack of suitable and affordable risk management services[16]
- Lack of appropriate livelihood financing, and

---

[14] The above services can be acquired through various institutions such as (but not limited to) the following: *Commercial and other kinds of banks including payments banks, non-banking financial institutions (NBFIs), cooperatives, credit unions, post offices, BCs/BFs, other MFIs, TELCOS and others who provide prepaid instruments* and so on. Not all services can be provided by all institutions though.

[15] An example is the bulk of what we typically call as priority sector financing with regard to MFIs in India, often coming under the micro-credit category. MUDRA loans are another example. See http://www.rbi.org.in/Scripts/BS_ViewMasCirculardetails.aspx?id=5818. There could be more relevant categories depending on quantum of loan, but these are the broad and most frequently used categories

[16] See a news item in the *Hindu Business Line* (May 22, 2012)—"We have found massive problems in insurance operations of SKS Microfinance", J Hari Narayan, chairman, Insurance Regulatory and Development Authority, told *Business Line*. "IRDA teams conducted field enquires and inspections for a long time, he said. The irregularities included receiving the cheques of death claims from its insurers on its name, which is illegal. The only listed MFI in the country, based out of Hyderabad, had also 'collected' higher commissions than permitted by the insurance regulator while selling the insurance policies." Source: Quoted from https://www.thehindubusinessline.com/money-and-banking/irda-finds-massive-problems-in-sks-micros-insurance-operations/article20436904.ece

- Low penetration of digital wallets and related services among low-income people.

Ninth, the focus needs to be on the critical issues of the quality and impact of financial inclusion, which have hitherto been ignored so far. Here, we need data on two important parameters: a) the quality of the financial inclusion services delivered; and b) how access to the various financial services have been of benefit to these mutually exclusive low-income individuals/households, small businesses and others? Both of these critical issues are very rarely talked about even globally, and transparent data on these aspects is almost non-existent! Both *quality and impact* are very important, and much wastage of precious national resources has occurred because of our lack of attention to these.

Therefore, it is about time that we started to understand the quality and impact of financial inclusion, with a focus on the following:

a) *Ease in accessing financial inclusion services:* How easy is it for a low-income individual/household or small business to access the concerned financial inclusion service(s)? What are the physical and psychological barriers to access? What procedural aspects and cost related issues (both affordability and transactions cost) prevent the financial inclusion service(s) from being accessed by the target segment?
b) *Compatibility of financial inclusion services:* How tailor made (adaptability) are the concerned financial inclusion service(s) to the needs of the

customers? Do the service attributes meet the needs of the customers? Are customer needs considered when financial inclusion service(s) are being developed and introduced?

c) *Actual usage of various financial inclusion services:* What can be said about the actual usage of the concerned financial inclusion service(s)? How regularly are they used? What is the frequency of usage? For what length of time are the various services used?

d) *Impact of different financial inclusions services:* What is the impact of the different financial inclusion services? Have they reduced vulnerability in the livelihoods of the customers or enhanced their ability to cope with crisis situations, life cycle events and emergencies? Have they acted as a consumption smoothing mechanism? Have they helped in improving productivity in their livelihood and so on?

While the first three aspects given above (ease of access, compatibility and actual usage) relate to the quality of financial inclusion services, the fourth one concerns the impact of financial inclusion. And it should be noted that these are just starter variables and not necessarily exhaustive.

Thus, financial inclusion services must be easy to access and should be compatible with the needs of the customer and if both of these are true, there will be greater usage of the concerned financial inclusion services (other than for the one-time services). It is under such circumstances that we can expect some tangible impact *(ceteris paribus)* on the livelihoods of the customer or productivity of the small business and so on and so forth. Therefore, unless we have some understanding about the quality of financial inclusion and the related issue of impact, making unsubstantiated claims about financial inclusion leading to inclusive growth is certainly not appropriate! And indeed, those stakeholders who are serious about financial inclusion as an instrument for achieving inclusive growth must now start to focus more on the 'quality and impact' of financial inclusion services! If indeed, we are serious about financial inclusion as an instrument for achieving inclusive growth, we must start to focus more on the 'quality and impact' of financial inclusion services, rather than just look at the mere numbers that we have so far been emphasizing!

Tenth, it has almost been 13 years since the global movement towards financial inclusion, and much water has flown under the bridge. Financial inclusion today, both in India and globally, has moved further beyond—in line with the digital revolution—to encompass what we call "digital financial inclusion". Digital financial inclusion is the new kid in town and, therefore, one has to ask the question: What has been the real impact of all of this—both financial inclusion and digital financial inclusion?

- Who gains from all of these financial inclusion efforts?
- How do the end-user clients feel about this?
- What, according to their perspective, is going well?

- What in their opinion is going poorly?
- What are the various impacts with regard to being financially included in a digital sense or otherwise? Are there short-term impacts? What are the medium-term impacts? What are the long-term impacts? *Most impact studies are donor funded or service provider sponsored.* We need to understand things as they are from the other side, the clients' side, in an objective and realistic manner.
- What difference does being included financially, in a digital sense or otherwise, make to the life and livelihoods of the end user?
- What are the problems, risks and issues (if any)—including client protection—that are exacerbated by the financial inclusion efforts, digital or otherwise?
- Is there a relationship been financial inclusion, digital financial inclusion, income inequality, poverty and livelihood security? What is it?
- Overall, who is benefitting from these financial inclusion efforts, digital or otherwise?
- From a future perspective, what needs to be done strategically and operationally to ensure that financial inclusion efforts (digital or otherwise) help address issues such as income inequality, poverty and livelihood security, as mandated in the SDGs?
- What can be said about issues pertaining to financial inclusion, digital or otherwise, from a regulation and supervision stand point?
- What practical lessons and suggestions are available from clients for all stakeholders,

including central banks, other regulators, service providers, donors and others?

Eleventh, another key aspect is the lack of a strong focus on agriculture as far as financial inclusion is concerned. No agenda on financial inclusion is complete if it ignores agriculture, which is perhaps the single largest occupation/livelihood provider for poor/low income people in India and many other agrarian economics. For example, providing a range of need-based financial services to over 600 million people engaged in agriculture (and related sectors/areas) remains a huge challenge in India, even today. And unless that challenge is successfully met quickly, in the already dualistic nature of our economy, the disparities will continue to widen between India and Bharat. Under such a situation, financial inclusion and inclusive growth will remain lofty objectives that have no feet on the ground. Let us be clear on that! And much of this applies to many other agrarian economies as well.

Similarly, after agriculture, the major employer is the MSME sector and financial inclusion of a range of MSMEs (including informal sector enterprises involved in agriculture and non-farm sectors) are critical for inclusive growth. It would be good to have a special focus on this important topic. Therefore, while inclusive finance, as a paradigm, has gained significant acceptance in India among policy makers and some others, and is being touted as the mantra for success, there are several good reasons as to why it has not achieved serious success on the ground so far. We have a unique opportunity to look at this critical issue and understand why this is the case. I am sure a major part of this would concern the manner in which the financial inclusion construct is treated—i.e., more as a static rather than a dynamic phenomenon.

Twelfth is the lack of specific focus on cooperatives, despite 2012 having been the United Nation's year of cooperatives. And cooperatives, despite all of their perceived weaknesses, are still the most vibrant community development financial institutions (CDFIs) worldwide, and yet they appear to receive much less attention in comparison to banks, NBFI MFIs[17] etc.

Last but not the least, the financial inclusion effort and the digital financial inclusion paradigm do not have a (strong) focus on client protection. Given what happened in Andhra Pradesh in 2010 because of MFIs, due to which large numbers of people still stand excluded, it would only have been appropriate to have had a specific focus on protecting clients in various models as they walk back through the first mile in the financial system. This is especially true of digital financial services, which are still in their infancy. Having said that, let us now focus on the technological innovations that are storming the financial sector—in their effort to include more people across countries—in chapters 5 and 6, which deal with blockchains and FinTech respectively.

---

[17] The term NBFI-MFIs is used to denote non-banking finance institutions (NBFIs) that are microfinance institutions (MFIs).

Chapter 5

Blockchains, What They Can Do for Financial Inclusion

In December 2017, a friend sent his American editor two hundred dollars[1] as fees for editing his book. The payment took six days to reach his editor via the correspondent banking network. Also, the editor complained that he received just one hundred and eighty dollars in his account. My friend was also harassed in trying to track the payment during the six days. This typically sums up what is happening in the field of international payment flows, especially using the decentralized correspondent banking network (and the current alternatives) which are costly (fees of four to ten percent, sometimes even higher), time consuming, and lack transparency in terms of payment tracking. Given the huge size of the cross-border flow market, which was greater than $ 190 trillion in 2017 (as per unconfirmed reports), we surely must look for alternative ways that are

---

[1] The term dollar always denotes the currency U.S. dollar, unless otherwise stated.

cheaper, faster and transparent. I believe that with a conscious coordinated effort, governments, central banks, financial institutions and several other stakeholders could be impressed upon to support a global blockchain-based[2] cryptocurrency plus solution to the problem I have stated above. This, however, calls for thoughtful design that can push policy makers and regulators to try something unconventional so as to reduce costs, save time and enhance transparency in cross-border payments. And mind you, this single step would go a long way in enhancing sustained financial inclusion and thereby propel us towards our goal of SDG 1.3—100% sustained financial inclusion by 2030.

To set the context right, let us be clear that the global financial system (GFS) is huge today, as it transfers several trillion dollars a day across billions of users. Predominantly, this GFS has many characteristics that make it undesirable. It is: a) inefficient with a lot of unnecessary costs built in via fees/charges, which gets further compounded by delays; b) outdated and old-fashioned, depending hugely on burdensome and

---

[2] A blockchain is an open distributed ledger that fundamentally acts as a database of (financial, legal, physical or electronic) assets that can be shared across a network of multiple sites, geographies or institutions. The most wonderful aspect is that all participants within the network have their own identical copy of the ledger. And any changes to the ledger are reflected in all copies—at the earliest within seconds and at the latest within minutes. The security and accuracy of the various assets in the ledger are maintained cryptographically through the use of 'keys' and signatures—this is to control who can perform what actions within the shared ledger. Entries can also be updated by one, some or all of the participants, according to rules agreed by the network, which often has multi-stakeholder governance.

superfluous paper driven processes, despite the shroud of digitization that appears here and there; c) centralized, lacking the flexibility, ability and willingness to respond to changing circumstances; d) hugely vulnerable to fraud, cyber and other crime etc (remember the *Equifax* case[3]); and e) not inclusive, as billions of people still don't have access to formal/basic/affordable financial services.

And the inefficient GFS has meant that regulatory (compliance) costs have started to rise alarmingly for all kinds of stakeholders. Even regulatory and supervisory authorities are overworked and overburdened. And all these manifest as higher costs for us—the consumers—who are forced to bear the brunt of this inefficient system. But I believe that a solution is in sight—i.e., blockchains. If appropriately designed, implemented and nurtured, blockchains can potentially help us overcome many of these problems.

The question is, who will play the lead in achieving this? Will central banks lead the blockchain revolution? What do blockchains mean for the banking industry? I don't believe that blockchains will foreclose banking. However, that said, it requires bankers/banks (as some have already started doing) to adopt the blockchain paradigm and use it in an innovative manner. However, I don't see banks

---

[3] See 'Equifax Says Cyberattack May Have Affected 143 Million in the U.S.', September 7, 2017, *The New York Times*, Tara Siegel Bernard, Tiffany Hsu, Nicole Perlroth and Ron Lieber, https://www.nytimes.com/2017/09/07/business/equifax-cyberattack.html

leading the blockchain revolution either in the financial sector space. Given that financial services and technology are getting married in a variety of ways, one could expect hybrids like FinTech firms to show the way. But, in my opinion, the real dark horses are the 'central banks' and I believe that when they realize the full and complete potential of blockchains, they will lead the blockchain revolution with certainty and clarity of purpose. In terms of timing, it could happen in 2018/19, sometime sooner rather than later. If you ask me why central banks and why not all other banks, I will tell you that banks won't lead the blockchain revolution, simply because a media house did not launch Twitter or a car manufacturer did not put Uber on the road or a TELCO[4] did not create Skype. Central banks are key (unexpected) stakeholders in the blockchain revolution because the potential for use of blockchains in financial regulation and supervision are immense indeed.

That said, what are some of the other benefits that could accrue from the blockchain revolution?

A problem that I have always faced with financial institutions[5] is the kind of outreach data they provide. There is so much overlap that it is almost impossible to decipher what the real outreach is. I

---

[4] TELCO is the sort form for a telecommunications company involved in the delivery of financial services. Examples include: *Vodafone* or *Safaricom* in Kenya, *Airtel* in India and other parts of Asia and so on.

[5] The term financial institution is used generically to denote a wide variety of financial institutions including different types of banks, NBFIs, cooperatives, credit unions and so on.

have found inconsistencies in the best global databases available, based on which I have presented my critique of their databases to the concerned stakeholders. Blockchains, which time stamp the data, offer potential solutions as the distributed ledgers are reconciled immediately and instantaneously, and also data is strictly immutable, in a sense. A ministry of finance or regulator sponsored permissioned blockchain for KYC (know your customer) requirements using biometrics coupled with data on various financial services could play a crucial role in helping to understand the real outreach and thereby bring in the much needed transparency.

KYC and anti-money laundering (AML) regulations cause delays for banks and increase their costs. The procedures are also a major obstacle for the people (especially the excluded) who have to provide a variety of documents if they are going to open a bank account and so on. I have personally found the documentation required very cumbersome. A blockchain, by providing a shared KYC/AML ledger to multiple banks/financial institutions in a region/country, can easily solve the problem. With such a system, just one bank would be required to onboard the client. The KYC information is then validated and recorded in the blockchain, along with the customer's identity. When the customer goes to a second bank, all that the new bank has to do is to look up the customer on the shared blockchain ledger and cross-verify the KYC information—then the bank account can be opened. The same process applies to all institutions (insurers, pension funds, etc.,) who require KYC/AML documentation. Any revision about the customer's KYC/AML status can be done by any of the institutions and it will be updated and reconciled immediately across the shared KYC/AML ledger and can be accessed by all in the permissioned blockchain (which is required to prevent fraud and misuse, that could happen in an open blockchain).

Now let us move to the tricky part—privacy and control of this data. What if all personal identity/KYC data (unique identifier, biometrics etc) are stored on a permissioned blockchain (as noted above) but the right of access is with us, the individuals. What if banks and other financial institutions can access this blockchain for KYC compliances only after we grant them access to the data? That would be great. Equally phenomenal would be the day when our banking transaction data, income tax returns, credit histories and key health data are stored securely, immutably and after time stamping on the permissioned blockchain, which we can grant through selective preferred access to: a) banks and various types of FIs for availing loans, opening savings accounts and fixed/recurring deposit schemes and making and transferring payments; and b) insurance companies for taking different types of insurance and the like. That would, in my opinion, represent real digital transformation through the power of a blockchain. It has great implications for financial inclusion and its measurement as well. I am sure the day is not far off when this will become a reality—huge benefits will accrue in cost as well as time savings, efficient operations, data with high integrity, privacy protection, and more.

The question that many of you will have is whether blockchains can help in keeping digital identity safe? My answer is a qualified yes. Recalling the data breaches (running into millions of customer accounts) that have occurred,[6] blockchain technology appears to offer a potential solution to many of the pressing digital identity (theft) issues as identity, I believe, can be distinctively authenticated in an indisputable, unalterable, and secure manner in blockchains.

Existing approaches, by and large, use the typical password-based systems of shared secrets swapped and stored on highly insecure systems. Blockchain-based authentication is based on indisputable identity verification using digital signatures that use public key cryptography. However, there is a catch—in blockchain-based identity authentication, the one and only check performed is whether or not the transaction was signed by the correct private key. And it is inferred that whosoever has access to that correct private key is the actual owner. In some ways, this means that the exact identity of the owner becomes irrelevant. That said, still, by a large measure, I feel that blockchains are perhaps better than conventional systems with regard to the protection of digital identity.

Ok, what else can be done on a blockchain?

---

[6] See 'That Yahoo data breach actually hit three billion accounts', October 4, 2017, *Wired*, Matt Burgess, https://www.wired.co.uk/article/hacks-data-breaches-2017

Can credit histories be put on a blockchain? The *Equifax*[7] hack has exposed the huge vulnerability (and associated suffering) of storing sensitive customer data on a centralized database. What really worries me is that we pay to have our credit history stored and companies cannot even protect our basic data.

As in the case of a shared ledger for KYC/AML that I mentioned above, why can't credit histories be stored on a shared ledger of a blockchain in which banks and financial institutions participate (i.e., update and access information). Apart from cost savings for all, other benefits are likely: a) Credit histories cannot be monopolized by any one stakeholder; b) It won't be (stored) in a centralized location that is vulnerable to hacking;[8] and c) Most importantly, the customer will be a part of the authentication process—i.e., whenever any stakeholder wants to access and/or use the credit history.

That, in effect, is a safeguard to privacy and also a safeguard against potential misuse. It is about time we have a serious rethink on how credit histories are stored, updated and accessed! Credit histories belong to us and we have a right to ensure their transparent, safe and fair use! Without a doubt, credit histories must be built into the blockchain using transactional data—the potential is great in terms of what can be done.

---

[7] *Ibid.*
[8] *Ibid.*

Discerning real leverage in the financial system becomes crucial for supervisors but in reality it is difficult because a lot of it stems from shadow banking activities and participants—both of which are complex to supervise and get transparent data on.

Even today, there is a huge problem in estimating the real leverage in the financial system because shadow banking activities and institutions operate in a complex, globally interconnected manner and, as in 2008, "leverage remains well disguised and hidden through derivatives positions, in off-balance-sheet entities and by 'window dressing' of financial reports."[9] Thus, comprehensive and transparent data on counterparty credit exposure between institutions in the financial system is still lacking.

Indeed, unless one is able to time stamp, aggregate and reconcile (in real time) multiple trading portfolios, one cannot get to know the real leverage. That is where blockchain technology promises a lot. Regulators must thus cajole financial sector participants to get their data on a permissioned regulatory blockchain. This should greatly contribute to unearthing real leverage and usher in an era of smarter supervision. And both of these should contribute to higher safety, soundness and stability of the financial system.

---

[9] 'Financial Crisis Inquiry Report, Final Report of the National Commission on the Causes of the Financial and Economic Crisis in the United States', The Financial Crisis Inquiry Commission, 2011, http://fcic-static.law.stanford.edu/cdn_media/fcic-reports/fcic_final_report_full.pdf

Algorithmic approaches to fraud detection, money laundering and so on are already being used by the private sector and regulators. For example, see the *Fedwire* tool—the Fed transaction analyzer[10] "helps financial institutions aggregate, save and analyze transaction data and assess potential exception activity, eliminating the time-consuming and error-prone manual processes related to risk management and compliance support procedures."

With blockchains/distributed ledger technology (DLT), this can get even better. DLT will enable banking regulators/supervisors to track in detail the evolution and history of every transaction on their systems—it means that the exact origin, final destination and utilization of funds can be traced without any doubt and in a precise manner.

DLT will also improve the ability of banking regulators/supervisors in identifying suspicious customers/groups and thereby help them in their efforts to identify/control systemic payment risks. This is indeed an area which the blockchain industry must take up seriously for policy advocacy in different countries with central banks, starting, of course, with (blockchain) supportive central banks like the Bank of England.

In fact, I was even exploring the implications of blockchains for a field such as accounting with a colleague. I argued as follows: Assume a transaction

---

[10] See 'FedTransaction Analyzer', https://www.frbservices.org/financial-services/bundled-solutions/fedtransaction-analyzer.html

occurs between you and I on the blockchain. It will be on a shared distributed ledger and the transaction will be cryptographically sealed, time stamped and immutable. This, in turn can provide reliable and valid (reconciled) data that has high integrity.

This is what auditors are supposed to produce at the end of the day and that is what regulators and supervisors want—indeed, a blockchain (if designed appropriately with the right checks, balances and smart contracts, etc.,) can produce that. Furthermore, audit trails can become completely transparent with full traceability. That is the beauty of blockchain technology. If thought through and applied appropriately, blockchains can greatly assist in getting near tamper-proof data (time stamped at the time of its creation) which is what regulators and supervisors in many industries require. Again, while it is still early days, the potential for cost savings due to automatic reconciliation can also contribute greatly to cost reductions in banking and other industries. Perhaps even smart (automated) audits could be possible. That is the potential—only time will tell whether it can be realized!

While the above are some of the applications of blockchains, what we require are institutions that are willing to try these efforts with innovative, intuitive and practical design, driven by people with good domain and technical knowledge. Blockchains promise to solve many of the irritants of the past decades and should be piloted and scaled up immediately for enhanced accountability in the financial services industry. Without a doubt, blockchains thus offer innumerable advantages, if designed and applied appropriately.

As noted earlier, one set of stakeholders who could be very useful in the mainstreaming of blockchain technology are central banks. It is important for the blockchain industry to get into policy advocacy with central banks. Policy advocacy must highlight the fact that DLT holds immense promise for enhancing regulatory compliance in finance and other industries globally and especially in a secure, low-cost manner. The role of DLT in KYC compliance has been highlighted already. And DLT is still dynamically evolving and, therefore, developers need to be given ample time to realize its complete innovative potential.

Having said that, we need to note that DLT as a technology is complex and regulators (whosoever they are) need to first understand it better. Indeed, that is why regulators must adopt an enabling plus wait and watch approach. First, they must form expert task forces to better understand DLT.

No doubt, DLT, like any technology, may have risks and could be prone to abuse, fraud or error, but given DLT's immense potential for enhancing regulatory compliance in many industries, regulators will have to take a very eclectic approach to its regulation, as the DLT also offers innumerable benefits for deployment and use as a compliance and supervisory tool, especially within the regulatory domain. And as a society, we simply cannot afford to lose these benefits and hence, heavy handed regulation of DLT cannot work and should not be deployed!

Thus, it is clear blockchains seek to disrupt and transform even the very (centralized) nature of institutions. And in the financial sector where financial services and technologies are coming together in rather unique ways, it is a matter of time before blockchains bring in quantum change in a manner that few of us can even imagine today.

The key to a competitive advantage in a blockchain dominated financial services industry should therefore lie in a firm's ability to adapt and innovate continuously, all the while assuming that the world of 'tomorrow' will be radically different from that of 'today'. In other words, financial services firms and FinTech companies must start to assume and anticipate that the very nature of the problem (that they are attempting to solve) could itself change fundamentally.

And this, in turn, calls for a complete change in culture and mindset, with a focus on disruptive and transformative innovation—the key to success should therefore lie in firms identifying newer problems to solve rather than just structuring solutions (to existing problems). As can be inferred from a reading of Miles and Snow (1978) and their typology of organizations, the world of tomorrow will be drastically different from that of today.[11] That

---

[11] See 'Organizational Strategy, Structure, and Process', July 1978, *Academy of Management*, Raymond E. Miles, Charles C. Snow, Alan D. Meyer and Henry J. Coleman, Jr.,

slogan is likely to be the mantra for success in a blockchain dominated financial services industry.

A key question that I have been asked several times is whether blockchains need to be regulated and if so, how. One aspect that I am sure of is that blockchains cannot be regulated in a rigid rules-based manner. Whether and how to regulate blockchains is itself a tricky question because blockchains can be used in multiple ways—for example, in financial sector regulation and supervision as a compliance tool. So, the real issue here is that when a blockchain is itself used for compliance by regulators, regulating blockchains becomes redundant. It is the blockchain technology and its attendant risks that need to be taken care of. Nonetheless, sound principles for multi-stakeholder governance (MSG, covering all risks in the use of blockchains) are required and need to be formulated immediately at the platform/protocol, application and ecosystem levels. That can form the basis for any future enabling regulation, if required.

Much as I hugely support blockchain technology, I also feel it necessary to highlight risks associated with it: a) It is generally considered impossible to decrypt records in the blockchain. I am not sure that this is a valid assumption with the kind of advances we have today in technology. Alternatively, what if someone buys off a stakeholder in the blockchain who has official permission to decrypt the records; and b) Yet another oft talked virtue is privacy. In reality, it may

---

https://www.jstor.org/stable/257544?seq=2#metadata_info_tab_contents

be possible to use transactions to get to the identity of a party—either through plain simple logic and deduction or with the connivance of a stakeholder who may have (official) permission to decrypt the data. There is yet another possibility, and this is precisely why we see permissioned blockchains—a ledger could be taken captive, provided one is able to assume control of a majority of the participating computers. Indeed, that is why blockchains concerning financial institutions and banks for KYC and other purposes must be permissioned blockchains, where only approved institutions are allowed access. So, neither security nor privacy can be taken for granted. Both of these must be properly managed through solid (multi-stakeholder) governance mechanisms at the platform, application and ecosystem level.

Ok, that takes us to the question on how to regulate DLTs.

DLTs possess a number of unique features that call for eclectic approaches to their regulation (if any). Let us understand these unique features first.

First of all, this mandates a deeper understanding of the legal issues that pertain to DLTs and I will deal with them, one by one. One key legal issue pertains to the territoriality, jurisdiction and application of concerned law—this is crucial, should something go awry in the blockchain. To the best of my knowledge, DLTs need not have one location, as different network nodes can be located across the world. This makes the pinning down of territorial jurisdiction and application of extant laws (naturally) difficult. It is possible to argue that each node will be governed by the extant laws of the country where the node is located but that clearly is a recipe for chaos and disaster, as reconciling extant laws from different contexts will be counterproductive and even impossible. This takes us to two questions: On whom do you pin accountability and responsibility, should something go awry in the blockchain? Who do you sue if something goes wrong, as there is no centralized authority? So, that's clearly an issue, along with the aspect of liability. We have to invent practical solutions that stimulate innovation and yet minimize risks.

Second, given all the data breaches that have happened with regard to digital identification,[12] I am now clear that DLT can solve the identity issue and store critical personal information safely. This is because of a key requirement—the need to be able to maintain information about each individual securely and transparently while not breaching their privacy.

This is where DLT scores, I believe. Look at the reverse issue—when we don't have DLT, it means that all the information is stored in a central depository. This can be disastrous, as we have already seen many times that a central depository can easily be attacked, changed, etc. To me, my digital identity

---

[12] See https://www.linkedin.com/feed/update/urn:li:activity:6312636898712092672/ and 'That Yahoo data breach actually hit three billion accounts', October 4, 2017, *Wired*, Matt Burgess, https://www.wired.co.uk/article/hacks-data-breaches-2017

and personal information is critical information and if I am going to give this away—I am talking about our most private, personally identifiable information—it jolly well be highly secure. While security is one issue, another is the need for a "de-identified identifier", where individual privacy can be protected. This is where DLT scores over centralized databases, in my opinion.

There has been some talk about computer codes (self) governing/regulating the blockchains. All that is fine but what we need to recognize is that computer code (in smart contracts) is law for machines but how can computer code be law for humans, who de facto control the machines and systems on which smart contracts run and blockchains operate. While the case for a wait and watch approach to blockchain regulation is strongly recommended, that does not mean that computer code will replace law in the regulation of blockchains or, for that matter, even governance of blockchains.

Let us not forget that while computer code is law for machines, likewise, legal law is the supreme code of behavior for the people behind the scenes, who are involved in operating these machines and systems. So, clearly arguing that blockchains must only be governed and regulated by computer code is inappropriate. MSG is required for broader governance of blockchains—at the platform plus protocol, application and ecosystem levels—which must again be based on some notion of legal law/codes of conduct. To reiterate, while computer code can be the law for smart contracts in an individual sense, blockchains can be governed/regulated only by legal law!

Let us take the case of the internet as a precedent for regulating blockchains. By and large, governments over the years have shown deep restraint and great foresight in regulating the internet. Here, I must emphasize the fact that it is the limited regulation of control over the internet by governments that has led to its burgeoning growth and development. Rules and regulations, if any, came in much later. Likewise, blockchains, which represent an internet of value plus information must be allowed to flourish and expand under MSG, rather than have any specific regulation. At a much later stage, as required, principles-based regulation can be brought in, rather than rules-based regulation. From a regulatory perspective, a principles-based approach does not use restrictive and prescriptive rules. Rather, it emphasizes broad principles to set the overall standards by which regulated entities have to conduct their business.

Again, I must re-emphasize that it is too early to think of any regulation for blockchains. We need to let the blockchain mechanism develop fully and wait and watch this development carefully, including manifestation of risks, if any. Development of standards with regard to MSG of blockchains is what is required urgently now.

MSG stands for the development of a governance model jointly by private sector, governments and civil society—using shared goals, principles, rules, decision-making, etc.,—that can shape the evolution and effective use of blockchains in different contexts and industries.

MSG has multiple levels of governance—platform level; application level; and larger ecosystem level. Platform level governance deals with individual protocols such as Ripple, Bitcoin, Ethereum or Hyperledger. Application level governance relates to tools—such as smart contracts—that run on these platforms and require huge coordination and collaboration between a number of diverse stakeholders. Ecosystem governance concerns the entire blockchain industry, encompassing various platforms whose protocols may or may not directly communicate with each other or be directly linked.

Just as we experimented with the internet and stabilized to have a good working model of MSG, the same will have to happen with regard to blockchains. And industry associations will have to play a catalytic role in setting standards for the development of MSG (at various levels of analysis) for blockchains—which represent an internet of value plus information.

Blockchains are the future and for a number of good reasons—transparency, immutability of records, global peer network, exchange of value, decentralization, secure record keeping, almost real time updates and reconciliation and so on. But as the technology develops, so must governance of blockchains. Agreed, power in a blockchain is dispersed and distributed but that does not imply 'no' governance. Indeed, MSG is what blockchains are about and for that we need standards. Without good MSG, blockchains may never realize their full potential.

Well, with increasing numbers of blockchain start-ups across industries, I guess the onus now lies on industry associations to play a catalytic role in establishing (initial) standards for MSG of blockchains. Here again, dynamic standards are required, as blockchains are still evolving. This drive for MSG should also get people to shed their cultural barriers and share information, data and power that they normally would not. Without a doubt, the key to good MSG lies in the transparent sharing of information and power across the blockchain in an efficient and equitable manner and industry associations must play a catalytic role in this as well.

To summarize, Miller and Friesen (1982) talked of quantum organizational change. James B Quinn (1980) spoke about incremental change. Blockchain technology fits into both of the above, as it is disruptive and transformative in nature. Blockchain is a vast, globally distributed ledger/database running on millions of devices. It is open to anyone, where anything of value—money, titles, deeds, music, art, intellectual property, etc.,—can be moved around, and stored securely and privately. On the blockchain, trust is established, not by large powerful intermediaries (read as banks, governments and technology companies)—rather, it is done through decentralized large scale collaboration and smart code. In blockchains, cheating and hacking are difficult. Blockchain technology, which excludes third parties during transfer of values, should result in quick, secure and private financial transactions that are also relatively lower cost—e.g., international remittances. Blockchains will democratize and expand the GFS, making it really inclusive—all the while offering, especially to those who are disadvantaged, higher quality access to financial services and payment systems that are more robust, fair and have a stronger defense against corruption, fraud and abuse.

Before I sign off, let me give an example. Take the case of small marine fisherfolk (SMFs) the world over. Regular and exotic varieties of fish are often exported but because SMFs are unable to establish traceability, their bargaining and negotiating power is very limited in the supply chain.

In India, for example, SMFs often have accounts receivable turnover spanning 2/3 months on the fish supplied and this affects their viability and livelihood. I talked to various stakeholders as part of an FAO/UNTRS (2008) study and lack of traceability was cited as a key issue for the various problems that SMFs faced, including not getting the kind of (low cost) credit that exporters got. The irony was that while exporters were eligible for packing credit at 6-9% annual percentage rate, the SMFs, who did all the hard work, often found it very difficult even to obtain formal credit. Worse, their accounts receivable turnover in the supply chain spanned over 2/3 months. I believe all of this can be sorted by designing an appropriate fisheries blockchain, which would permit traceability and also offer many associated benefits to SMFs including enhanced livelihood options by way of making them eligible for formal (non-subsidized) credit at lower cost etc. A blockchain should also help contribute to sustainable fishing practices in the long run.

Blockchains are thus the future and they create greater transparency and accountability. Financial services for low income people can have far greater outreach, enhanced access and much lower costs if they adopt blockchain technology. Likewise, infrastructure and logistic applications (including smart contracts) of blockchains are mind boggling in terms of their efficiency benefits. To ignore blockchain technology would be a huge mistake. They are here to stay and it is more a question of when they take over rather than if, as blockchains represent an internet of value plus information as opposed to a mere internet of information.

Chapter 6

FinTech, Digitization and Digital Divide

The world development report (WDR, 2016) talks of a global digital divide of almost 60%. How to enable these potential users to cross barriers imposed by literacy and language and make better use of digital technology to conduct financial transactions?

But before we get to solutions, let us first look at the obstacles to digital transformation and the transition to a cashless (or less cash) economy: (1) Lack of mobile data and internet connection and financial (process and digital) literacy, especially at the grassroots; (2) While people may have bank accounts, these need to be used regularly and continuously; (3) There are many vested interest groups that do not desire a shift towards a cashless economy and they need to be countered; (4) In emerging and developing economies where small (MSME) retailers tend to dominate, investment credit with regard to electronic payment infrastructure must be available; (5) Consumer perception also acts as a barrier. The benefits of cashless transactions are not clear even to those who possess credit cards. Alternatively, cash is generally viewed as a superior and quicker method of transacting. There is also a belief that cash helps a person negotiate better. All of these need to be changed; and (6) Lastly, most consumers (including card users) carry the impression that they might be charged more when they use cards (instead of cash). This perception also needs to be changed. Without a doubt, all of these need to be tackled expeditiously by countries that desire to move forward rapidly with regard to digital transformation.

Given the above context, in terms of solutions, if you ask me honestly, I feel the strong need for an artificial intelligence (AI)-based, voice-led FinTech application that will help users negotiate mobile banking systems, undaunted by language, digital and process literacy. Two issues dominate the design of such a system: a) The fact that sections of the population that still remain excluded from digital financial systems are still handicapped by a lack of comprehension of the (financial) processes and their workings; and b) The need for digital and process literacy to these people to be imparted, on the go, before they can effectively use the available solutions. The key point to note here is that traditional classroom-type training cannot work effectively here. Training the users, especially the lower rung of low-income people, at best, has to be a parallel process if the users need to be enabled to get on the digital bandwagon straight away. That is why an AI-based voice-led application—that can handhold the user through the transaction and other processes is necessary. In this case, users will be guided by a 'virtual voice', in the language of their choice, every step of the way, telling them what to do. Technology can thus be an enabler!

Thus, while FinTech is still very nascent, as applications of AI, machine learning and deep learning become common place, the ability and potential of FinTech to serve large numbers of low-income people and the poor is huge. Let us make no mistake about that. FinTech must be well supported by central banks through an enabling developmental regulatory framework as it has significant potential to eliminate commonplace frauds, enhance outreach and deepen access. FinTech can do a lot to enhance financial inclusion and lower actual costs of delivery.

The potential of distributed ledger technology (DLT) for facilitating regulatory compliance is also huge. In short, FinTech, in its true, full-grown avatar, will disrupt and transform traditional banking and financial inclusion paradigms like never before and let us welcome and usher in a true FinTech revolution with open arms. Indeed, what we are seeing now is just the tip of the iceberg and there is a lot more that needs to happen if FinTech is to become a game changer and push us further forward towards achieving 100% sustained financial inclusion by 2030 as per SDG 1.3.

Having said that, let us ask what FinTech can do for financial stability. Decentralization (and diversification) in the financial system can reduce the effects of financial shocks in most situations. Put differently, the failure of a single and specific kind of firm is less likely to close down the entire financial system—of course, when a large set of systemically important institutions go bust and financial markets are globally inter-connected, then, as in the U.S. subprime (of 2007/8), a lot of devastation can be felt.

That said, the larger point is that decentralization and diversification, to a large extent, can mitigate the impact of financial shocks. And therefore, one could argue that FinTech, which leads to greater decentralization and diversification, can indeed have a positive impact on financial stability. As an example, the application of DLT could reduce concentration in the settlement process.

The flip side of the argument is also possible as economies of scale and scope could lead to greater concentration in certain situations. Indeed, this concentration could result in the increase of nontraditional financial service providers (of systemic importance[1]), who, in turn, could have a (negative) impact on the ability of the financial system to recover from shocks, thereby undermining financial stability.

---

[1] Without a doubt, these nontraditional service providers of financial services must have appropriate mechanisms for general governance (see chapter 9 of this book), governance of compensation (see chapter 10), governance of risk management (see chapter 11) and independent internal audits (see chapter 12).

That said, while I am all for regulatory support to FinTech services, monitoring the quality of internal control of such innovative technology becomes critical. While who should do that is one question we can all debate (in terms of regulation versus self-regulation), what mechanisms must be used to judge the adequacy of internal controls is something that is rather clear. And given the financial crisis that happened in 2007/8 in the United States (subprime) and spread globally, it is imperative that we focus our attention on four basic aspects related to internal control (especially if these technologies are dealing with people's money):

a) Does the technology's control environment embody the principles of strong internal control?
b) Whether the risk assessment system in the technology allows for responding to existing and emerging (including political) risks.
c) Has the technology established effective control activities across its entire spectrum of functions?
d) Whether the accounting, information, and communication systems embedded in the technology ensure that risk-taking activities are within established policy norms and whether these systems have been adequately tested and reviewed.

The above four aspects are critical from the perspective of financial stability and safety. Additionally, all of these FinTech institutions must have the governance, risk management, compensation and internal audits standards set out in chapters 9, 10, 11 and 12 of this book.

Moving on, let us ask what drives FinTech. Answering this question should also tell us how FinTech would be able to ramp up our efforts to financially include excluded people and thereby contribute to achieving the goal of 100% sustained financial inclusion by 2030 (as per SDG 1.3), provided a wide range of need-based products and services are delivered in a fair, efficient, affordable and sustainable manner.

In my opinion, FinTech is driven by three critical factors:

- *Customer preferences:* Millennials and others who have grown up with digital transformation have exhibited a strong preference for FinTech because of the multi-faceted convenience, swiftness and overall (lower) cost of gaining access to financial services.
- *Technological innovation:* Burgeoning growth of appropriate technology—related to artificial intelligence (machine and deep learning), internet, mobile technology, big data, raw computing power, etc.,—has enabled new-age technology driven financial institutions (FinTech) to deliver specific financial services at a much lower cost than traditional ones. This technology has also permitted quicker scaling up of these FinTech institutions as compared to traditional financial institutions (FIs) and banks.
- *Regulation:* After the 2007/8 financial crisis, regulatory requirements have become more stringent and this has led to the growth of non-traditional intermediaries for financial services.

These eclectic FinTech companies have started to replace the traditional banks/FIs, who have to contend with far more stringent capital requirements and greater compliance costs. And hidden leverage is perhaps now more under the supervision radar, forcing the traditional banks/FIs to go in for greater deleveraging and reduced lending.

What then are the critical issues in FinTech?

a) What is the regulatory domain and how to circumscribe it with regard to FinTech?
b) Does it require updating?
c) How to manage operational risks from third party service providers (such as cloud and big data entities) who could be concentrated in another region or country? How to set minimum governance, risk management, compensation and internal audit standards and disclosure guidelines for such entities?
d) How to manage transnational legal issues and regulatory arrangements? How to ensure seamless communication between regulators within and across countries?
e) How best to get the private sector on board to facilitate wider sharing of lessons at this nascent stage? Constructive dialogue with the private sector is necessary and central banks must provide a bias-free platform for this.
f) How to enhance central bank and regulatory and supervisory staff capacity with regard to FinTech? Even if resources are available, what skills sets are necessary on a graduated basis? And how soon

and where can they be acquired to keep pace with the burgeoning growth of FinTech?
g) How best to mitigate the ever-expanding cyber risks? As FinTech expands, even one weak link in the chain is enough to break it.
h) How best to accommodate digital currencies and understand that they are legitimate and here to stay?

Having said this, let us ask the question, what kind of regulation is necessary for FinTech companies, in terms of principles- versus rules-based regulation? While the debate can be endless, given the nascence of the FinTech domain, I would strongly argue for a principles-based approach that uses a broad set of standards and nudges market participants towards a set of specific desirable outcomes—in terms of governance, risk management, compensation and internal audits.[2]

These are more suited than rules-based regulation that permits the mere checking of boxes for regulatory compliance. At the end of the day, FinTech entities should be made to feel that they are responsible for outcomes and consequences and will be judged by that rather than by strict rules, which can be restrictive and complex. Safeguards must of course be there, that goes without saying.

As the union of technology and finance gets better and better, we are drawn by the hope of near 100% permanently inclusive financial systems and

---

[2] See chapters 9, 10, 11 and 12.

accordingly, it may be more useful for players in new innovative fields like FinTech to become accustomed to broad principles-based regulations rather than the restrictive rules-based ones. Hope central banks will lead in this aspect conclusively and settle for principles-based regulation with regard to nascent fields like FinTech.

Going deeper, I see one of the key issues of operational risk in FinTech concerns how regulators and supervisors deal with third party service providers (such as those in cloud computing and data services including big data) who are becoming more critical for operations. This problem becomes compounded when all the FinTech companies use the same third party service provider or the same set of third party service providers. There are implications for financial stability.

This gets even more complicated when these third party service providers are outside the ambit of the regulatory domain. And the problem gets accentuated even more when these third party service providers are in a foreign country, bringing in cross-border issues. Specifically, it remains to be seen as to how regulators and supervisors can maintain effective oversight on governance, risk management, compensation, internal audits and other aspects related to these third parties. That is indeed a critical issue.

Clearly, regulation and supervision of FinTech is not straightforward and must be approached with innovativeness, practicality and a deep knowledge of finance and technology domains. A related question here is whether regulators or supervisors in central banks have the skills, knowledge and resources to deal with FinTech. This question needs answers because only then can they (regulators or supervisors) make a fair assessment on whether or not FinTech-led financial services (including banking) is likely to affect financial stability.

A crucial starting point for central banks, therefore, is to first acquire this much needed capacity, as FinTech promises a lot in terms of enhancing financial inclusion. For this, central banks must understand what the risks from FinTech are and how these can be mitigated—something which requires one to work at the critical union of technology, finance and innovation. And indeed, how regulators and supervisors acquire these skills and knowledge is indeed a crucial aspect that will determine the fate of full-fledged FinTech-led financial services (including FinTech banking) in the days to come.

One another point is in order here—the question of how FinTech-led financial services can build the trust of end users, customers and other stakeholders alike needs strong focus, as does the issue of consumer protection. The trust factor is all the more important for FinTech products as they are replacing tangible currency with abstract digital money. So, they need something to build trust and a voice interface can surely help.

FinTech companies can do two things: 1) Have artificially intelligent FinTech applications that can talk, listen, interact (in the native mother tongue of the customer) and thereby wow them during the delivery of FinTech products and servicing of customers; and 2) Have a no-frills simple toll-free number that people can easily (emphasis added) access (in their own native mother tongue) to solve their problems with the FinTech-led financial service and process. This will greatly enhance the trust of low-income people in FinTech and also enhance client perception of customer protection mechanisms available in the FinTech industry—both of which should immensely help us in meeting our goal of 100% sustained financial inclusion by 2030 (as per SDG 1.3).

And last but not least, FinTech can greatly step it up by helping to deliver vulnerability reducing and bargaining power enhancing financial products, especially in the field of agriculture and value chain financing, which are topics discussed in chapters 7 and 8.

Chapter 7

Financial Inclusion and Agriculture

In countries like India, in particular, farmer suicides and agrarian distress has been occurring for decades and yet, we continue to: a) pour more money into agricultural finance (with no quality credit); b) offer loan waivers; and c) enhance minimum support prices. Yet, the puzzle has not been cracked and farmers continue to be in crisis. Much of what I say in the context of India[1] applies to other agrarian economies as well.

Indeed, the agrarian crisis continues and seems to be getting worse! Why?

---

[1] I will use the example of India to illustrate the key issues here as India is one of the largest agrarian economies worldwide.

Because the real issues are not being addressed—be it strategic, operational and other issues at the grassroots or the (gaps in) key linkages between agriculture, finance, and agricultural marketing. Without a doubt, solutions can be found but not by piecemeal strategies. We need to deal with this comprehensively and offer practical solutions that can mitigate (and perhaps in the medium to long term, eliminate) farmers' distress.

Let me start with an example from India, and I hope that the financial institutions[2] involved in this space attempt to redress the same. I also hope that the central bank looks into this issue so that the tripartite contract farming products become more sensitive to the needs of low-income clients and are indeed fair to them. And while the problems described affect all farmers, the effect on marginal/small farmers is much higher as they do not have diversified sources of income.

Specifically, I take the case of sugarcane farming, and illustrate the need for available financial products to be made more client-sensitive and responsive. Financial inclusion of sugarcane farmers[3] is typically undertaken through contract farming in India, with tripartite agreements between the financial institution,[4] sugar

---

[2] The financing institutions typically include a wide range of entities (banks, NBFIs, cooperatives, credit unions, etc.,) that lend to typical low-income people, small and marginal farmers, microfinance clients and so on.

[3] There are said to be over 40 million sugarcane farmers in India and another 50 million people are supposedly dependent on this industry for their livelihoods. The same tripartite model is a vogue in several other agrarian economies too.

[4] The financing institutions typically include a wide range of entities (banks, NBFIs, cooperatives, credit unions etc) that lend to typical low-

factories and clients. While the financial institutions[5] are the real drivers of this financial inclusion arrangement, often the sugar factories, which provide the inputs and technical assistance, also play an important role.

Consider a marginal sugarcane farmer like Ramaiah (in the Madurai district[6]) who has 2 acres of land. The story of Ramaiah symbolizes what a typical small sugarcane farmer goes through. Ramaiah was financially included when the cane supervisor in a major sugar factory approached him in 2007 and asked him to grow sugarcane in 1.5 acres of his 2-acre land with a perennial well. Under this supposedly inclusive tripartite contract farming arrangement (between farmer, sugar factory and bank), the factory was to supply the inputs, provide technical assistance and buy back the sugarcane; the bank was to provide the loan for buying the inputs, including seeds and fertilizers, and the farmhands to cultivate the crop and earn returns.

Ramaiah was a small farmer who grew vegetables and the family labor of four people was sufficient to get out the vegetables in time and to the nearby town market. While Ramaiah did not make much money from vegetables the year round, there was at least one season in a year where he would reap bumper returns—due to

---

income people, small and marginal farmers, microfinance clients and so on.

[5] The financing institutions typically include a wide range of entities (banks, NBFIs, cooperatives, credit unions etc) that lend to typical low-income people, small and marginal farmers, microfinance clients and so on.

[6] This district is located in the state of Tamil Nadu in India.

marriages being plentiful, lower produce coming to the vegetable market during the period of heavy rains in October/November, and other factors.

Ramaiah was clearly sold on the sugarcane idea suggested by the cane supervisor of a sugar factory, who had argued that the sugarcane crop (and intercrop of onions) could help him generate handsome returns. But alas, that was not to be and Ramaiah's experience with sugarcane farming, like that of many (small/marginal) farmers across the country, is one of complete disaster. Having received a bank loan, he barely managed to make any money, post-harvest, from the first sugar crop. The ratoon[7] crops were bigger disasters in subsequent years, and today, the bank is proceeding against him for recovery of dues and he is excluded from the financial system, as are many others like him who took to sugarcane farming.

What are the causes for this? Ramaiah says that the whole tripartite (financial) inclusion arrangement is structured against farmers like him, for several reasons.

First, the sugarcane setts (seeds) supplied to him (as part of the loan) were over-mature and hence, germinations were low and a lot of gap filling[8] had to be done. Ramaiah asks, why should he pay for gap

---

[7] Ratooning is a practice of harvesting a monocot crop. This is done by cutting most of the above ground portion but leaving the roots and growing shoot intact so as to allow the plants to recover and produce a fresh crop the next season. That way, one can have multiple cycles of crops—second, third, fourth and so on but with progressively diminishing yields.

[8] This would include the cost of the replacement seeds and labor for planting these.

filling when poor sugar setts were supplied by the sugar factory in the first place?[9] To understand this, consider the following example. Normally, 35,000 sugarcane setts can be planted in this acreage. Assuming a germination of 60%, the farmer will have to gap fill the remaining 40% of the setts again, if he/she is to get a decent yield. The population is the key to getting a good yield; but to maintain population,[10] the farmer has to gap fill and often unilaterally bear the cost. And more often than not, for a variety of reasons beyond the farmer's control, the setts supplied do not germinate fully.

As part of the arrangement in contract farming, the farmer gap fills the sugarcane setts (in case of poor germination) and he/she bears the cost of poorly germinating seeds, which is typically added to the loan. Thus, the farmer bears the burden, despite the fact that poor germination often occurs because poor setts were supplied by the sugar factory (mainly due to supply of more than mature setts, or immature setts, or setts from a ratoon sugarcane crop and often caused by factors beyond the farmer's control). Please note the fact that the cost of gap filling is always

---

[9] The sugar factory has control of the sugarcane setts supplied as it cuts the standing sugarcane from (other farmers') fields specified as sugar setts (seeds).

[10] For example, 35,000 sugarcane setts are typically planted in an acre. Each sett has 2 eyes and this makes it 70,000 eyes in 1 acre of land. Each eye grows to become a shoot weighing approximately 1 kilo in 11/12 months, depending on the variety. If 70,000 eyes germinate (100% germination) and each of them reaches 1 kilo in 11/12 months, then the farmer gets a yield of 70 tons per acre. If there is 60% germination, then the yield is 42 tons per acre (70,000 setts x 60% germination x 1 kilo = 42 tons) and so on. *Therefore, maintaining the sugar sett population at a high and optimal level, is crucial to getting a good yield.*

invariably borne by the small producer, even if poor setts (seeds) have been supplied by the sugar factory. The sugar factory is the key player here because it decides which farmer's crop will go for seed, when it will be cut and supplied, and the like. Therefore, under the tripartite financial inclusion arrangement, the onus for the quality of setts (seeds) is almost entirely that of the sugar factory.

A *second* reason Ramaiah mentioned was lack of fertilizers, microbes (like Rhizobium) and tonics on time, which means that there are huge delays in fertilizer application. Ramaiah argues that, as he found out later, while the complete loan interest ticks away from the date of signing the agreement with the financial institution[11]/sugar factory, the supply of ingredients (included in the loan) by the factory is neither on time, nor of the specified quality. He argues that time is of the essence in sugarcane farming and when that critical time is passed, no matter how much extra fertilizer is given, the growth of the crop will falter. He also complains he had to do extra weeding before the late fertilizer application as weeds had grown again in the intervening period.

A *third* issue Ramaiah mentions is that the sugarcane must be cut at the appropriate time, and here again, there are delays in cutting orders from the sugar factory. In his case, he argues that the cane was cut when it was overripe, and hence, there was a huge loss

---

[11] The financing institutions typically include a wide range of entities (banks, NBFIs, cooperatives, credit unions etc) that lend to typical low-income people, small and marginal farmers, microfinance clients and so on.

to him. He argues that undesirable (corrupt) practices prevail here and those who pay money get their cutting orders earlier.

A *fourth* reason is the aspect of cut cane being lifted after significant delay, as a result of which the cane weight comes down and there is loss to the farmer. He argues that nefarious practices in transportation effectively increase the lead time from when the cane is cut to when the cane is transported and delivered to the factory. In his case, the cut cane was allowed to lie on the ground for over two days and this meant significant moisture loss (and perhaps sugar content), as a result of which there was considerable weight loss and consequent yield and revenue loss for the small farmer. In fact, he cites that this is a very serious problem for small farmers, as the contractors arranged by the sugar factory for transporting the cane from the farmer's field to the sugar factory insist on bribes/bata and '*baksheesh*'[12] to lift the cane. If farmers do not comply, they leave the cut cane to dry in the field and this can seriously reduce the yield and resultant return for the farmers.

Likewise, there are many other instances of problem situations in cultivation, where marginal/small farmers are hit quite badly. The larger point is just a simple one- the financial product is simply not sensitive to the needs of the small farmer and it perhaps even penalizes him/her for the 'wrongdoing' of other parties. Poor seed supplied by the sugar factory could cause lower germination, but the gap-filling cost is always that of

---

[12] *Baksheesh* is a bribe.

the farmer. The machines in the sugar factory could stop (due to failure/fault) and as a result, the cane of the small farmer cannot be unloaded, and thus not weighed at all—there are many cases where the small farmer has lost almost 50% of weight and resultant revenue because of lorries not being weighed for 3 to 4 days.

Now, despite all these (manmade) odds, the small farmer/producer has to repay the loan with interest. And if he[13] cannot, he becomes 'untouchable' and gets excluded from the formal system, often never to get re-included again and left to the mercy of 'infamous' moneylenders. And more often than not, financial institutions (including banks and other formal institutions) use the joint liability group mechanism to ensure that the loans taken get paid by guarantors—even when the yield from the sugarcane crop is reduced (due to the unfair actions of other stakeholders) and, therefore, the income from the crop is insufficient to pay off the loan.

What needs to be noted here is that the interest on the loan starts ticking from when the agreement is signed and/or the seeds are supplied to the farmer, whereas payment is made to the farmer at least three to four months after the crop has been harvested and supplied to the sugar factory. And when you factor in the delays in supplying the fertilizer, cutting the crop and/or lifting the cane to the factory, you realize that the

---

[13] This is true for all types of small producers, including silk weavers in Kanchipuram or Malda/Murshidabad, different kinds of artisans across India, fisherfolk in the south Indian peninsula and several others about whom I will be writing in the future.

sugarcane farmer is a modern day Karna,[14] who is killed many times before the loan (Arjuna) overwhelms him.

In some ways, the above financing arrangement is outrageous as it penalizes the small producer for the mistakes of the other parties in the arrangement, which reduces yield and revenue. The fair thing to do would be ensure sharing of the risk and costs among the three parties—i.e., producer, sugar factory and financier. This would enable alignment of incentives and ensure that there is congruence in all actions and inputs.

In fact, Ramaiah's case and that of other similar small farmers/producers has tremendous implications for financial inclusion in this country.

- Financial inclusion is a necessary but sufficient condition for better livelihoods. Those who attempt to include the poor and disadvantaged must also pay attention to other factors and risks that can result in the included being ultimately excluded again. This is a very significant lesson for those arguing for financial inclusion of the poor—

---

[14] In *Mahabharat*, a great Indian epic, after Arjuna (of Pandavas) kills Karna (with the Kauravas), he tells Lord Krishna, I am so sorry that I killed my brother. Lord Krishna says that Karna died many times before and what Arjuna did was to merely send a last arrow. Karna was also considered as the epitome of sacrifice and loyalty. The metaphor is used here to show that there are many places where unfair practices do the equivalent to included Indian sugarcane farmers and thereby makes them default on their loans and get ultimately excluded. Much of the same logic applies to other agrarian economies as well. For example, I saw the same kind of exploitation of farmers in St Lucia, Uganda, Kenya, Malawi, Philippines, Indonesia and elsewhere.

through livelihood financing—as a means rather than an end.
- Finance (livelihood or microcredit), as it currently exists, is not fair to the client or small producers. Hence, finance must focus on quality servicing and attempt to be sensitive to clients' needs and design/deliver products that are fair and useful to them. More improper finance could only be disastrous and this is one of the main reasons as to why we see a cycle of inclusion and exclusion among low-income clients. In fact, that is why newer programs are perhaps being initiated time and again, including the present financial inclusion drive.

- Much more than financial inclusion needs to be done to ensure that farmers (and small producers) who put in the effort, make the investment and take the risk, actually get rewards and returns commensurate with their efforts, investment and risk. If this becomes the goal of financial inclusion, then properly delivered enabling services will automatically become a part of the whole financial inclusion agenda. This indeed has significant implications for the design of the wider financial inclusion program in terms of what they are doing and what they should be doing. I hope there is honest introspection in this regard and programs are tailored accordingly to meet the needs of low-income farmers and producers.

As a beginning, we could take up the cause of low-income sugarcane farmers and producers worldwide—a single client-sensitive, financial product would ensure that a large number of low-income people are indeed prevented from getting excluded. And the same analysis to ensure fairness to clients can be initiated with a variety of livelihood-related, financial products for low-income people. *These rather than any interest rate subsidy or subvention or loan waiver would serve the cause of financial inclusion and inclusive growth better.* I hope that ministries of finance and central banks in the respective countries[15] focus on ensuring fairness in financial access, which is vital to creating and sustaining inclusive growth in the world today.

Let me make it clear that I am not trying to blame anybody. What I am trying to do is point out that we have not addressed structural problems in the markets for agricultural produce, which continue to remain imperfect. More credit (at even 0%) to agriculture will simply *not* help. Rather, what we need is credit that will reduce vulnerabilities, and help small producers overcome various kinds of risks caused by imperfect markets. A greater deal of emphasis has to be placed on post-harvest financing, especially the appropriate kind and at a sufficient scale for the bargaining, staying and negotiating power of smallholder producers to be enhanced, especially in the wake of imperfect markets for agricultural products. We need financial inclusion and FinTech to help small producers and farmers in combating the vulnerabilities and risks posed by imperfect markets.

---

[15] Countries which are strong on sugarcane farming include the following: Brazil, India, China, Pakistan, Thailand, Mexico, Colombia, Indonesia, Philippines and the United States.

Indeed, inequality is a fundamental problem and it requires solid reforms with regard to the structural issues that lead to inequality in the first place. Inequality arises primarily because of imperfections in the intermediate and final markets for agricultural products/labor and so on. The key to tackling inequality—which is the world's foremost problem today—lies in creating structural solutions that break the vicious cycle of market imperfections and ensure that agricultural markets operate in a fair, equitable, transparent and accountable manner. And financial inclusion and FinTech can show the way by creating reformist paradigm change, driven through fundamental structural solutions that can make agricultural markets fairer and equitable. And all of this must be done at a sufficient scale so that rising global inequality is tackled in a fast and expeditious manner.

Yet another puzzle that we have not been able to fully crack globally are the returns from agriculture in general, and for small/marginal farmers in particular. Exceptions apart, by and large, returns are still relatively poor across the globe for agriculture in general (which is why it is so heavily subsidized even in the west). While pilots seem to work, well-meaning projects end up in a perpetual pilot testing mode and scaling rarely takes place. Ask yourself this question—when is a farmer (especially small/marginal ones) most vulnerable? Post-harvest obviously, as they are sitting with a perishable, whose weight dwindles by the day. Clearly one solution lies in creating competition for the purchase of agricultural produce post-harvest. Agriculture finance can play a great role in creating this competition (post-harvest) by eclectic financing of the purchase of agricultural produce. But for this to work on a large scale, structural reforms will have to take place and governments will have to demonstrate the political/administrative will to take on cartels. Only then can the negotiating/bargaining power of farmers be enhanced and will returns from agriculture be decent.

Providing financial services to millions of people engaged in agriculture and in the agribusiness in poorer and remote rural areas, remains a huge challenge in many countries, including India, even today. And unless that challenge is successfully met quickly, in the dualistic nature of our economy the disparities will continue to widen. Under such a situation, financial inclusion and inclusive growth will remain lofty objectives that have no feet on the ground.

While some might argue that the growth of the microfinance sector has led to significant breakthroughs in performance, outreach, and lending volumes, this has rarely extended to low-income people in remote rural areas, dependent solely on agriculture. And, as the microfinance experience largely suggests, financing by institutions[16] has primarily tended to be consumption related; although some of them have provided small production loans to low-income people.

In fact, you can count the number of MFIs[17] who have looked at agriculture financing in a serious way. And

---

[16] The financing institutions typically include a wide range of entities (banks, NBFIs, cooperatives, credit unions etc) that lend to typical low-income people, microfinance clients and so on.
[17] BASIX, an NBFC, is one such rare example in India.

given the 2010 microfinance crisis, it is clear that mere consumption loans can do little to financially include low-income people, let alone those involved in agriculture.

While the importance of financing agriculture to promote inclusive growth in India is well appreciated, we first need to understand why ensuring sustainable financial access for successful agricultural production and rural enterprises development has always proved difficult. The often cited constraints are, (1) high transaction costs for both (borrower) producers/enterprises and lenders; (2) high risks faced by both of them, and especially covariance risk for agriculture; (3) the lack of reliable production/financial data and other information with regard to rural households engaged in agricultural and rural enterprises; and (4) financial products ill-suited to the cash flows and livelihoods of the borrowers.

While the above constraints are genuine and perhaps require more than just financial access, the key point is that access to financial services can play an enabling role and help to address many of these constraints. The underlying assumption is that improving the provision of, and access to, financing for agriculture can indeed prove critical not only for the success of agriculture, but is also vital for promoting inclusive growth, as very large numbers of people are still dependent on agriculture for their livelihood.

So what can be done in a practical sense to re-engineer financing of agriculture?

For this, financial inclusion of agriculture should not be merely viewed as enhancing access to finance for primary producers in an agriculture value chain, but rather, it must be seen as a broader intervention that can, (a) help create better and enabling infrastructures in the chain; (b) enhance competition among various stakeholders and increase choice within the chain; (c) reduce vulnerability of producers (marginal, small and primary producers) and increase their staying/bargaining/negotiating power vis-à-vis other actors in the chain; (d) act as a catalyst and stimulate access to productivity-enhancing technology and practices; (e) facilitate small/marginal and other primary producers to get better returns/rewards through better access to business development services including markets; (f) enable product, process, functional and channel improvement/upgrading in the chain, which is very critical; and/or (g) address other constraints/challenges that small and marginal producers face, and the like.

In practice, such a broader outlook with regard to financial inclusion of agriculture is likely to enable achievement of the larger development objectives, such as ensuring inclusive growth in a more effective manner.

Some of the specific aspects that such financial inclusion could focus on with regard to such agriculture financing is given below.

- *Repositioning agriculture and rural life*—this calls for priority focus on access to finance in agriculture in terms of investment credit, risk mitigation products and finance for infrastructure, including watersheds, extension services, quality inputs, standardization and the like, apart from and most importantly, finance for marketing of agricultural produce.

- *Promoting innovation, competitiveness and growth of agribusiness*—competition-enhancing finance for players in various agriculture supply chains (mainly middle level) and especially for other kinds of intermediaries (like producer organizations). This apart, there could be specialized financial arrangements for the re-structuring of such supply chains and the like.

- *Strengthening agricultural health and food safety systems*—it is critical to do this in terms of inputs, processes and infrastructure and ensure that various standards are adhered to. Finance for infrastructure is important here and offers a great opportunity.

- *Introducing appropriate technology and innovation for the modernization of agriculture and rural life*—again, innovative financial products can play a major role here in bringing technologies from lab to land in a successful manner and facilitating their wide-scale adoption by small producers and farmers.

- *Strengthening existing agricultural and rural communities*—enhancing the staying and bargaining power of small and marginal farmers is going to be critical. Thus, finance for reducing the vulnerability and risks of small producers would be most useful, and this alone will enable them to participate fully as stakeholders and demand and get their due. This would include a range of post-harvest financing arrangements, including warehouse receipts.

As several stakeholders have argued, agriculture is indeed at a crossroads and a major challenge is to reverse the present trend of slow-medium growth in most developing country contexts, including India, and push it in the high growth path/trajectory.

The key seems to be to provide an integrated set of services, including access to financial services including credit, access to market, value adding technology, training, access to machinery, storage facilities including warehouses and cold storage, access to extensions, processing facilities and quality control.

Partnership between public, private sector companies/organizations and, most importantly, communities is needed in order to provide these integrated services in a seamless fashion at scale and profitably.

Overall, any efforts towards financial inclusion in agriculture must strive to improve the bargaining power of smallholder producers, while also reducing the transaction costs for intervening stakeholders through promotion of truly democratic producers' groups, associations and cooperatives. Small producers will be able to effectively participate in the changing markets and establish links with new market actors (agribusiness companies, processors, exporters, chains, etc.,) only if they have access to basic infrastructure, quality inputs and various services, they are organized, and most importantly, empowered in terms of staying power and bargaining power. All of this, of course, requires quality, innovative and vulnerability—reducing financial services of a sufficient scale, and not just the traditional micro-credit or conventional agriculture financing.

In fact, there is a clear need to look closely at most, if not all, agriculture value chains in the country from the primary producers' perspective and re-engineer financing arrangements to enable and facilitate a wide range of innovative financing solutions that can reduce the vulnerability of the primary producer. I hope that the concerned ministries and stakeholders, including the ministries of finance, ministries of agriculture, central banks and other stakeholders in the respective countries[18] take up this task on a war footing that is critical, if indeed they are serious about fighting poverty and ensuring that there is inclusive growth for millions of low-income people (especially, small and marginal farmers) and that their dreams are powered for a strong, resilient and sustainable future in line with SDGs 1, 1.3 and 10.

One final point is in order here. The way forward for agriculture is 'smart agriculture' that combines crucial (good) elements of low external input sustainable agriculture, eclectic financing of agriculture, especially through vulnerability reducing and bargaining power enhancing financial products and information technology. If this is done along with the financing of

---

[18] Countries which are strong on sugarcane farming include the following: Brazil, India, China, Pakistan, Thailand, Mexico, Colombia, Indonesia, Philippines and the United States.

all stakeholders in a variety of agriculture value chains,[19] it won't be long before we realize the true potential of agriculture.

---

[19] See chapter 8 for key issues related to value chain financing.

Chapter 8

Value Chain Finance Can Power a Billion Dreams!

Value chain finance (VCF) has become a buzzword and you hear it everywhere today in the development field and especially in the agriculture sector—which has long been the primary economic activity in many countries in Sub-Saharan Africa as well as Asia. However, ensuring financial access for successful agricultural production and rural enterprises development has always proved difficult. Often cited constraints are: (1) high transaction costs for both (borrower) producers/enterprises and lenders; (2) high risks faced by both of them and especially covariance risk for agriculture; (3) lack of reliable production/financial data and other information with regard to rural households engaged in agricultural and rural enterprises; and (4) financial products ill-suited to the cash flows and livelihoods of the borrowers.

In fact, given the above, the last decade has seen VCF being promoted as 'the' approach to promoting access to finance for agricultural and rural enterprises. It is certainly not new and has had many previous avatars. And oftentimes, VCF is introduced in a very narrow sense, without a broader understanding of the specific sector and this leads to minimal impact, and ultimately, VCF is seen as a fringe activity. There have been numerous attempts in Asia and Africa, where a naïve introduction of a 'special' VCF effort has been lost and never to be tried again. I will try to capture some salient issues and lessons from value chain failures (I believe that failures teach us more than successes), without naming the specific projects/attempts.

VCF is typically defined as a flow of financing within a sub-sector, among various value chain stakeholders, for the specific purpose of getting product(s) to market(s). This definition mandates relationships and commensurate exchanges between value chain stakeholders through vertical and horizontal linkages, as well as coordination/cooperation and competitive mechanisms. This is very different from the mere provision of conventional financing, where one of the chain stakeholders (for example, a specific firm/entity and often primary producers) gains access to financial services independent of other stakeholders.

Given the above broader perspective, experience suggests that the first necessary aspect while getting into value chain finance is to ask what is really expected of it? That is critical. And accordingly, the most practical step would be to identify the constraints and gaps that could potentially limit the sector's capacity to generate the desired objectives, which, among others things, could include: a) vulnerability reduction for primary producers; b) better and stable returns to various chain actors; c) productivity increases in the chain; and d) higher employment generation across the chain and the like.[1]

This apart, the regulatory environment at the local, national, regional and international levels need to be factored and analyzed while looking at gaps and constraints in the value chain.

Thus, VCF should not be merely viewed as enhancing access to finance for primary producers in a chain but rather, it must be seen as a broader intervention that can: (a) help create better and enabling infrastructure in the chain; (b) enhance competition among various stakeholders and increase choice within the chain; (c) reduce vulnerability of producers (marginal, small and primary producers) and increase their staying/bargaining/negotiating power vis-à-vis other actors in the chain; (d) act as a catalyst and stimulate access to productivity enhancing technology and practices; (e) facilitate small/marginal and other primary producers to get

---

[1] This can be done by asking questions such as those given in the appendices.

better returns/rewards through better access to business development services including markets; (f) enable product, process, functional and channel improvement/upgrading in the chain, which is critical and taken up later in the appendix; and/or (f) address other constraints and the like. In practice, such a broader outlook with regard to VCF is likely to enable achievement of the larger development objectives such as ensuring inclusive growth in a more effective manner.

How can we use re-engineered value chain financing to enhance the bargaining power of small/marginal agricultural producers?

1. As noted previously, the mere delivery of credit and more of this standard credit (for consumption and/or small production needs), as is currently practiced in microfinance (or as part of the financial inclusion paradigm) is not always very useful—as low-income people in many contexts, like in India, and other similar countries (Uganda and Malawi in Africa) are engaged primarily in agriculture.

2. The focus would need to be re-engineered towards ensuring *delivery of quality credit* that will reduce the risk and vulnerability of low-income clients engaged in agriculture and give them more choices—through alternative channels that have lower costs, greater trust and high levels of mutual acceptance.

3. Quality credit would therefore necessitate a greater focus on post-harvest and/or post-production financing for agriculture and related sectors that provide (or can provide) significant livelihood opportunities for low-income people.

4. In other words, among other things, this would call for financing of agricultural produce marketing—a critical aspect for small/marginal producers as it has the potential to enhance choices for them in terms of buyers, etc. Of course, here, existing relationships would need to be better understood if financial products are to be developed and delivered through the appropriate channels.[2]

5. Furthermore, the re-engineering must be such that the delivery of financial services are used to strategically drive higher rewards, better remuneration and greater power down the value chain as shown in **Figure 8.1** below—otherwise, it will be of limited use.

---

[2] Of course, this would need to be validated specifically for a context, product and partner but these are general suggested arrangements.

Figure 8.1: Tracking Power and Influence with Value Chain Analyzes—Example of Agriculture

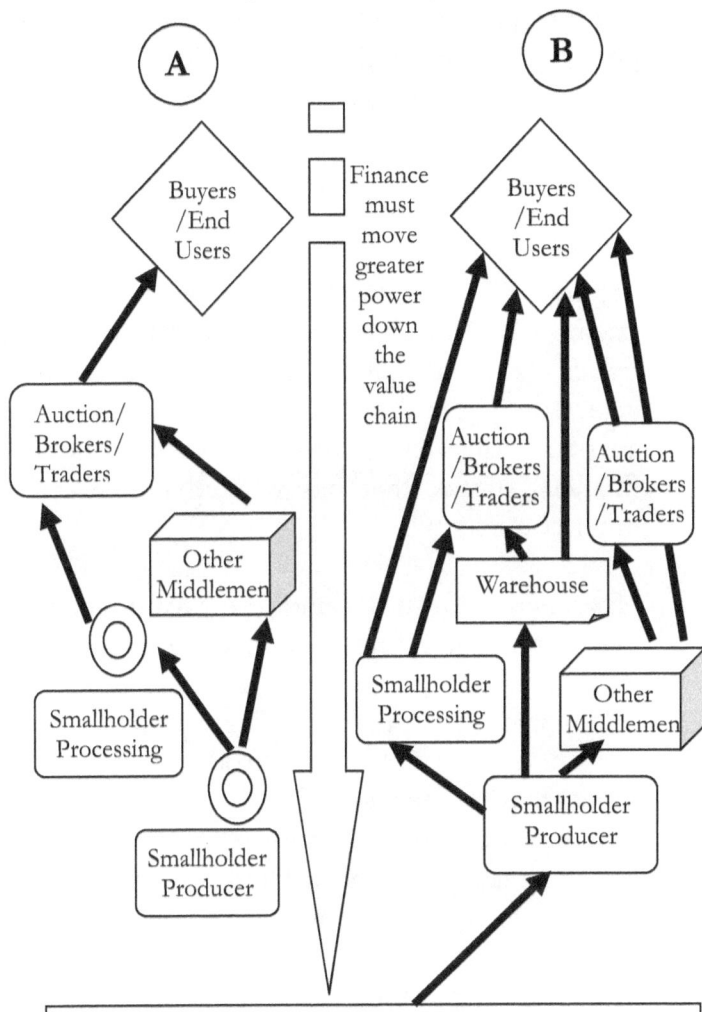

More power and reduced vulnerability for small producers in Scenario B as opposed to Scenario A, as finance gives them staying and bargaining power, reduces their risks and enables them to get rewards/returns commensurate with the value they create, the risk they bear, the investment they make and the effort they put in. Please note that there are an increased number of players in situation B as opposed to A and there are more choices for the clients in situation B.

6. And again, as said before, to achieve this, one needs to better understand the existing relationships, particularly in the post-harvest and post-production marketing situations in different agriculture value chains.

7. An example of driving power down the value chain is the delivery of finance through a simple warehouse receipt mechanism, as diagrammed in **Figure 8.2** below. While there have been attempts to do the same in India, large-scale frauds in small pilots have proved to be a deterrent. These should not, however, force us to abandon this excellent vulnerability reducing financial service that has worked rather well in other contexts:

"Experience from around the world illustrates that warehouse receipts can make a difference to producers. By storing their goods in a reliable warehouse until the price increases while using the goods as loan collateral, producers may access funds before they sell their goods. Warehouse receipts are often administered to producer groups, instead of individuals, which helps the flow of market information.

Warehouse receipts can also create price transparency. This empowers producers to make informed sales decisions rather than waiting for 'gate' buyers, who often offer below-market prices. Producer organizations and a range of financial institutions (including MFIs) also have a strong incentive to offer warehouse receipt financing. With this system, their risk is reduced because the system has a built-in use of collateral that can retain a high commercial value and be liquidated quickly."[3]

Figure 8.2: The Warehouse Receipts Financing Process

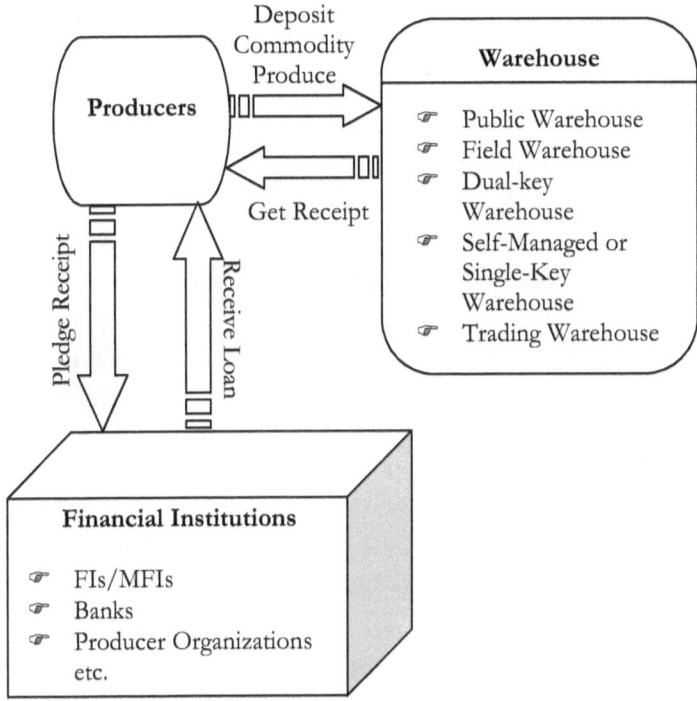

8. Thus, there must be re-engineering to emphasize the delivery of financial services that can enhance competition among middlemen and other buyers, who buy products/produce/labor from small

---

[3] Quoted with adaptation from UNTRS/FAO (2007), Arunachalam Ramesh S et al, 'Enhancing Flow of Finance to Small Scale Marine Fisheries' and Bamako 2000: Innovations in Microfinance, Technical Note 5.

producers. This would translate to financing the marketing of agricultural produce and the labor of small-scale producers[4] and it can happen in a variety of ways (through various types of aggregators and channels). Some examples are given below:

a) *Enhancing competition among buyers:* Direct financing of middlemen and other intermediate buyers of produce/products[5] so that small producers have a greater choice of buyers and incentivizing these middlemen to procure at better prices/rates;
b) *Risk and vulnerability reducing mechanisms:* Warehouse receipts and similar financing for other products whereby the small producer can store their produce/products, pledge the same, receive a loan and sell when the prices are higher. An example is leasing for urban vendors whereby they can store their produce on a daily basis at a cold storage facility and not sell their perishable item at a throwaway price at the end of the day, just because they have no place to store it safely and, being a perishable, it could get spoilt;

---

[4] Some of these would apply to fisheries as well, where post-harvest financing would be critical. Much of the same would be applicable for tangible goods and here again, the focus would be to create a good supply of post-production financing and creating competition among buyers of produce/products made by small-scale producers. Likewise, in the case of labor, innovative financing mechanisms like a livelihood finance exchange using the web could be explored.

[5] BASIX tried this in the initial years but again we need to study why it could not be scaled up and thereafter try and create an environment for the success of such mechanisms.

c) *Creation of post-harvest competitive mechanisms:* Financing of other post-harvest mechanisms including special depots for auction so that small producers have choices—this has happened in small-scale marine fisheries and the South Indian Federation of Fishermen Societies has successfully used auctions and other mechanisms to help the fisher folk get better prices
d) *Other strategies:* Financing of small-scale producers who use labor for their livelihood through an innovative mechanism like a virtual livelihood exchange, with appropriate aggregators, etc.

Thus, to summarize, we need a new approach to financing agriculture value chains and one that is rooted strongly in practical realities. With all due respect to everything that has been achieved, let's face it that the livelihoods of those in agrarian/rural sectors (in many agrarian economies[6]) especially are in great shambles—the fundamental point being that to build the livelihood security of small producers/farmers, there is an imperative need to reduce their vulnerability and risks, while at the same time enhancing their bargaining and staying power. And well-designed financial services can play an important part in that.

As an experienced colleague remarked, "Irrespective of the sector, small producers are not getting rewards/returns commensurate with their effort put

---

[6] India included.

in, investment made, risk taken and value created, mainly because their staying and bargaining power is low. It is therefore very important to try and promote interventions that enhance the staying power of small producers—as it will then result in their having better bargaining capacity which, in turn, will mean that they can negotiate better with market elements and get the return or price that is due to them."

This can surely be attempted by the financial services sector and it should pay rich dividends to both traditional as well as new age service providers and their clients—thereby helping to power a billion dreams, if not more and enabling us to reach the goal of 100% (sustained) financial inclusion as per SDG 1.3 in a quicker manner.

Chapter 9

Good Governance Critical for Sustained Financial Inclusion

Often, people look at the high-profile membership of the board as a surrogate for good corporate governance. But, despite having the equivalent of five-star boards, many financial institutions (FIs)—both traditional as well as new age ones—have come under attack for various weaknesses in governance. Interestingly, much of this is said to have happened, despite many of these FIs having what bystanders would often call a five-star board—that is, a board packed with well-known personalities from within and outside the industry. And indeed, this is where a common judgment made with regard to corporate governance has, often repeatedly, proved costly, both in the financial inclusion industry and the broader financial sector. In fact, if you look at the credit rating reports, this is apparent. These reports use the presence of a five-star board to claim that governance in these FIs is very good. Yet, as the past several years have shown, there were several controversial governance-related issues in many such FIs, as espoused by the following:

a. Inadequate checks and balances over executive decision-making and whimsical behavior by the board and/or senior management.
b. Insufficient transparency about ownership and control and related-party transactions.
c. High stakes acquired by promoters' friends/well-wishers/families in order to maintain control over the FI.
d. Lack of truly independent and nominee directors and board nomination subcommittees, conflicts of interest at board, senior management and operational levels, and other such aspects.
e. Lack of transparent reporting to the outside world.
f. Manipulation of processes regarding board functioning.
g. Non transparency in process of allotment of shares/options.
h. Insufficient transparency about the (FIs/group's) operational strategies and overall financial position.

Therefore, with the mere presence of a five-star board, it cannot be assumed that there is good corporate governance at the FI. The regulatory architecture must provide sufficient incentives for facilitating good corporate governance, while at the same time creating disincentives for bad governance. *This point needs strong emphasis.*

What is really interesting to note is that all of the corporate governance violations listed in the earlier chapters have happened, despite the concerned FI boards having so-called strong independent directorial representation on their boards. *Therefore, using board membership as a surrogate for good corporate governance is fraught with danger.*

In fact, the very premise of good corporate governance hinges on the ability of independent and nominee directors to act impartially, objectively and with prudence, keeping in mind the overall vision of the FI and its duty to all of its shareholders.

And sadly, this did not happen, as independent directors in many of the FIs lacked accountability and true independence in their functioning. Some of them were even compensated for by way of stock options and the like—instruments that compromised their independent functioning. Further, as many of them owed their appointments to the promoters/CEOs, this perhaps seriously limited their ability to function independently.

Strangely, even directors nominated by institutional investors were quiet and, sometimes, they did not even write a dissent note when the board norms and procedures were seriously violated. As an aside, it must be noted that the current procedures adopted by institutional investors to ensure the accountability (and effective functioning) of their nominee directors also appear rather weak. I will not go into the specifics, but there are numerous examples of situations (at FIs) that could have been salvaged, had the independent (and nominee) directors acted independently and truly in the interest of the (minority) shareholders.

Never mind, and let bygones be bygones. But going forward, the various concerned stakeholders would do well to ensure that there are clear regulatory (supervisable) standards with regard to appointment, roles, compensation and evaluation of independent directors, so that corporate governance in FIs does not exist merely on paper. This is one place where the regulatory reform for responsible finance could begin in earnest. *The various specific issues that would have to be looked into by them are highlighted here:*

- *Practice of CEO hiring board/independent directors in many FIs:* First, in many FIs, the promoter who is (often) also the CEO hires the board and this practice needs to be questioned from the perspective of implementing corporate governance directives on the ground. The key question here is whether a board hired by the promoter/CEO (of an FI) can really be independent in terms of its functioning? And the related issue is how such boards can be expected to perform the roles that they are supposed to in terms of safeguarding the interests of various stakeholders, including minority shareholders. So, this is an aspect worthy of regulatory attention.

- *Definition of an independent director:* Second, there is lack of clarity on who is an independent director in terms of objective criteria such as age, expertise, and experience, as well as having had past relationships with the same FI (which can result in significant conflicts of interest). Therefore, regulatory guidelines regarding the definition of independent directors would be very useful.

- *Appointment of independent directors:* Third, it seems appropriate to vest the powers of appointment of new, independent and executive directors in board nomination committees (at FIs), which must be a mandatory requirement for all types of FIs. These committees should follow a transparent process and lay down clear steps and criteria for selecting board members. Further, an independent director must chair the board nomination committee so that 'truly' independent candidates are hired to the FI board, and the climate for their 'real' independent functioning is ensured.

- *Time spent by independent directors on work at FIs:* Fourth, is the issue of whether independent directors should be mandated to spend a certain minimum time working at the FI and especially in the field at the operational level. As an industry observer argues, *"independent directors should be made to devote a certain minimum number of hours every quarter (or regular period) so as to understand the business and gain insights about the FIs in which they are serving as directors. This will enable them to examine the risks being taken and the appetite of their FI to take such risks as well as understand and provide guidance on other strategic aspects, as may be required."* This again could be looked into as part of the regulatory architecture.

- *Number of FI boards on which an independent director can serve concurrently*: Fifth, a related aspect is the amount of time spent by independent directors on board meetings at FIs annually. When there are people who, at any one point in time, serve as independent directors on several FI boards, the quality of directorship is naturally likely to suffer. It may therefore be appropriate to recommend a threshold level for the number of FIs in which people (professionals) could serve as independent directors. This is a critical aspect indeed.

- *Peer appraisal of independent directors must be made mandatory*: Sixth, peer appraisal of independent directors is an option for enhancing their effectiveness in working, and this, again, needs to be examined from the perspective of independent directors in FIs. While such an appraisal process would need to be managed with associated sensitivities, board members should also view this as an opportunity for continuous learning and improvement. Traditional methods of evaluation (in terms of share valuations/prices and strategy initiatives) would perhaps need to be augmented by a formal and objective appraisal of the independent directors' performance with regard to governance (in terms of various parameters). Such an appraisal should enable identification of gaps in governance, enhance the decision-making process and improve the effectiveness of board meetings and various processes at the FI. This is also an aspect that could be looked at in the context of FIs by the concerned stakeholders.

- *Capacity building of first-time (independent) directors*: Seventh, another critical area often ignored is the need for continuous education programmes for independent directors, especially for entry or first-time (independent) directors.

- *Compensation of independent directors*: Eighth, the compensation of independent directors is a critical issue and there have been a lot of controversies in recent years. Surely, there must be guidelines for the same so that the real independence of the independent directors is not compromised under any circumstances. One option would be to entrust this task to the board nomination committee and ensure that the promoters/CEOs do not interfere in setting and implementing norms of compensation for independent directors.

- *Protecting client interests on the FI board*: Last, but not least, the stakeholders should also examine whether there could be specially designated independent directors, representing client interests. We have directors in banks representing staff interests and the same could be done to safeguard client interests. Similar to compensation, this is an important issue in FI governance.

Thus, while enhancing the quality of independent directors would surely enhance governance, there is also a right mindset aspect that we should not forget. And the governance ecosystem must encourage and incentivize people to have the right mind set.

Therefore, the least we can do is incentivize good governance and, perhaps, penalize bad governance, and do this consistently and without fear or favor. For this, we need a practical guiding (regulatory and supervisory) framework pertaining to the appointment, roles, responsibilities and compensation of independent directors in FIs as noted earlier. Mind you, this is something that the financial service sector (in many countries) needs desperately as it is rather low on its governance quotient, because of the repeatedly occurring past crises and events.

You may wonder why I have dwelt so much on the topic of independent directors. One of the most critical reasons for the importance attached to the topic of independent directors in any organization (including FIs) relates to conflicts of interest. There are several issues here: (i) Conflicts of interest hinder judgment and affect decision-making; (ii) judgment and decision-making are what directors are asked to do; and (iii) directors must feel free to think, express, question, and decide in the interest of those they represent. And all of these apply very much to FIs as well, who, during the past few years, have received a lot of (negative) publicity with regard to corporate governance, conflicts of interest and the role of independent directors on their boards. In fact, the debate has now widened to encompass not only the roles of independent directors but also that of nominee directors from FIs, and several questions continue to be raised regarding real and potential conflicts of interest on the ground.

As noted above and earlier, while we highlighted corporate governance violations from past crises with regard to FIs and also outlined suggestions from a regulatory standpoint, let us also remember that FI boards can play a major role in fostering good governance on the ground. Here are some practical suggestions based on experience:

1. *Limit the number of FI boards on which a director may sit to not more than three at any given point in time.* This will hopefully afford directors the time and space to understand how the FIs, on whose boards they serve as directors, are actually performing on the ground. Therefore, it appears necessary to ensure that there is a limit—in tune with physical reality—on the number of FI boards in which a director may sit. And three to four appears to be a good permissible number to start with.

2. *Separate the functions of the chairman of the board of directors and MD (or chief executive officer or equivalent) in FIs where they are together, and ensure that appropriate outsiders occupy at least one of those posts.* This is critical and should result in dispersed power, especially when the founder promoter is the chairman and/or managing director. Much of the excessive risk taking that occurred during the lead up to the past crises happened primarily because

there was no one on the board to seriously question the enthusiastic and entrepreneurial promoters/CEOs occupying one or both of these positions.

3. *Create a transparent board **recruitment** (or appointment) policy that clearly specifies the duties and profiles of the FI directors, including the chairman.* Such a policy must also ensure that directors have adequate skills and experience (apart from the availability of time to do their job). The policy must also ensure that the overall composition of the FIs' board of directors is suitably diverse—including more women, youths, clients (or their interest groups), and individuals with the requisite skills (but possibly different backgrounds) in the board is perhaps a way to improve the boards' overall functioning and effectiveness. The policy must also ensure that conflict of interest issues are taken into account with regard to board appointments, so that the independence of the directors is not compromised.

4. *Ensure that FI boards develop (on their own) a formal conflict of interest policy and an objective set of **compliance procedures** and processes for implementing the same.* Such a policy should ideally include: (a) an FI director's duty to avoid (if possible) all activities and transactions that could either create a conflict of interest or even the appearance of a conflict of interest; (b) a transparent set of processes and procedures for FI directors to follow before they engage in certain types of activities (such as agreeing to

serve on the board of another FI or that of a lender or an investor, etc.) so as to ensure that such activities will not create a conflict of interest; (c) an FI director's duty to disclose any activity and issue that may result, or has already resulted, in a conflict of interest; (d) an FI director's (voluntary) responsibility to abstain from voting on any matter where the director may have a conflict of interest or where the director's objectivity/ability to properly fulfill duties to the FI may be compromised; (e) adequate procedures and clear norms for transactions and activities conducted with related parties on an arms-length basis; and (f) transparent procedures by which the FI board will deal with the issue of any noncompliance with the (conflict of interest) policy. Ideally, it would be good for the policy to contain specific (conflict of interest policy) examples of where and how conflicts of interest can arise when serving as an FI board member. This should facilitate greater understanding of conflict of interest issues, with regard to financial services delivery in general and the FI in particular.

5. *Have a compulsory formal evaluation of the functioning of the FI's board of directors by an external independent evaluator.* This is a critical issue and the results of this evaluation should be made available to shareholders and supervisory authorities—officially publishing this evaluation (on their website) is an aspect that could also be considered by the FIs concerned. This formal evaluation of the board should preferably be done in the

absence of the CEO or managing director, so as to ensure that the exercise is a free, fair, and independent one. The services of independent evaluators—individuals and/or institutions who have not had (or do not have) a material relationship (as defined in common parlance) with the FI—could be taken in this regard. Management institutes (such as IIMs) and others (like the College of Agricultural Banking, etc.) could also be actively involved in these (evaluation) processes.

6. *Suitably compensate FI board members for their time but do not incentivize their working on the basis of* **stock options** *or other such mechanisms that invariably encourage undue or excessive 'risk' taking, as was witnessed during the past crises.* Even if the law permits this, it seems prudent not to remunerate board members through stock options and the like, as the independence of (independent) directors may be seriously compromised. Past crises clearly demonstrate the fact that independent directors who had been so compensated had *not* performed their fiduciary and other duties appropriately. The key issue to note here is that many of the crises occurred because board members and senior management were compensated heavily (in the short term), whereas the risks of their strategies could be known only in the medium/long term. This mismatch created a huge incentive for excessive risk taking, which, in turn, led to the crises.

7. *Make it mandatory for FI boards to set up a risk committee and establish clear rules regarding the composition and functioning of this committee.* In addition, make it compulsory for one or more members of the audit committee to be a part of the risk committee and vice versa. Further, the chairman of the risk committee should always report to the annual general meeting (AGM) and outline the role that directors have played in shaping the FI's risk profile and strategy. Also, the risk committee should frame a 'risk control declaration', which should also be published so as to ensure its wider dissemination and use—both within and outside the organization.

8. *And last but not the least, create an obligation for a specific duty ('duty of care') to be established for the board of directors so that they take into explicit account the interests of various stakeholders (mainly, clients) during the decision-making procedure.* This is especially critical and the past crises would (perhaps) not have occurred, if only boards of FIs had exercised such a duty of care that explicitly looked after the interest of clients. Therefore, there is an explicit need to incorporate a duty of care—especially with regard to clients—among FI boards.

To summarize, for the financial services sector that has experienced many a crisis, corporate governance has never been more important than now. Corporate governance is not just the responsibility of an individual FI. Rather, it is the collective responsibility of all the individuals who become directors on the boards of an FI and serve together. While we can have great sounding norms and guidelines for corporate governance, unfortunately, they cannot be effectively enforced through regulation alone. They need to be practiced at all times (including difficult circumstances) and that is where the individual initiative of directors (serving on FI boards) does really matter. And I sincerely hope that directors on FI boards ensure that this happens in real time on the ground—by enabling and facilitating their boards to reorient their functioning in the light of the suggestions made.

If this happens, many of the ills plaguing the financial services sector and FIs will slowly but surely start to vanish and 100% sustained financial inclusion by 2030 as SDG 1.3 will be an achievable goal. It goes without saying that along with good governance, good practices in compensation and risk management are also critical for the traditional and new age FIs (especially FinTech entities) in their march towards 100% sustained financial inclusion by 2030 and these critical aspects are discussed in chapters 10 and 11.

Chapter 10

Governance of Compensation Necessary for Preventing Financial Exclusion

Governance of compensation played a very important role in the 2007/8 financial crisis that unfolded in the United States and spread worldwide. As the final report of the Financial Crisis Inquiry Commission (FCIC) notes,[1] "Both before and after going public, investment banks typically paid out half their revenues in compensation." Firms also paid out huge compensation even when they made losses. "For example... Merrill paid out 141% in 2007—a year it suffered dramatic losses. As the scale, revenue,

---

[1] 'Financial Crisis Inquiry Report, Final Report of the National Commission on the Causes of the Financial and Economic Crisis in the United States', The Financial Crisis Inquiry Commission, 2011, http://fcic-static.law.stanford.edu/cdn_media/fcic-reports/fcic_final_report_full.pdf

and profitability of the firms grew, compensation packages soared for senior executives and other key employees. ...That year Wall Street paid workers in New York roughly $ 33 billion in year-end bonuses alone. Total compensation for the major U.S. banks and securities firms was estimated at $ 137 billion."[2] In effect, in all these firms, the focus was on short-term performance, incentives, and compensation, when, in reality, the risks (which existed) were mostly medium and/or long-term. This performance—risk mismatch which led to unrealistic compensation is something that we should neither forget nor repeat— that is a key lesson in the governance of compensation for the financial inclusion industry.

As we have moved on from the financial crisis of 2007/8 (but are still recovering from its aftermath), there are several important lessons here with regard to the governance of compensation generally and in the larger financial sector (in particular) that we all need to understand and come to terms with. *Much of this holds true for the financial inclusion industry as well.* I will try and articulate some of these here for the benefit of various stakeholders. All of these are critical aspects that must be followed by financial institutions (FIs) involved in pushing the frontiers of financial inclusion in many countries globally. Additionally, ministries of finance, central banks and

---

[2] 'Financial Crisis Inquiry Report, Final Report of the National Commission on the Causes of the Financial and Economic Crisis in the United States', The Financial Crisis Inquiry Commission, 2011, http://fcic-static.law.stanford.edu/cdn_media/fcic-reports/fcic_final_report_full.pdf

financial sector regulators must also ensure that the following aspects are adhered to by FIs in respective countries, as otherwise compensation is one factor that could lead to a financial crisis and thereby cause exclusion of the very people we want to financially include:

Lesson #1: Lack of arm's-length decisions and negotiations: The governance of remuneration and incentive systems seems to have (apparently) failed because the decisions and negotiations (carried out) were not at arm's length. Conflicts of interest at various levels have aided such improper decision-making and negotiation, and much of this is applicable to the remuneration and incentive systems for a range of senior management personnel and not just the CEO or managing director or chairman of the board. While there are several examples from the 2007/8 financial crisis, the final report of the FCIC offers good factual insights. There are numerous examples in the case of microfinance institutions (MFIs) that were at the center of the 2010 Andhra Pradesh (AP) microfinance crisis as well.

Lesson #2: Inordinate levels of influence of senior management in establishing remuneration schemes: In my opinion, senior management generally appears to have had far too much influence over the level and conditions (including measures) set for performance-based remuneration. On the other hand, boards were often unable to or, sometimes, even incapable of exercising objective, independent judgment. Here again, there were serious conflicts of interest, which certainly exacerbated this whole issue—in fact, this has been one of the most important reasons for inaction by the board against inappropriate remuneration proposals of senior management at many of the institutions at the center of the 2007/8 financial crisis. Much of this again applies to MFIs at the center of the 2010 AP microfinance crisis as well.

Lesson #3: Medium and long-term risks are not taken into account: In many cases that I have closely observed, the relationship between performance and remuneration has been rather tenuous and, sometimes, even difficult to establish, especially given the nature of the operations. A critical aspect here is that medium as well as long-term risks were rarely factored into the whole process—something that should have been done naturally. How can rewards be in the short-term, when the risks are medium-long term? Again, there are numerous examples from the subprime crisis and the 2010 AP microfinance crisis.

Lesson #4: Complicated and opaque remuneration schemes: The remuneration schemes have also been fairly complicated and opaque, in terms of shrouding the actual conditions in the operation of the scheme and the consequences. These (operational conditions and terms) are perhaps not clear and obvious to the naked eye of an unassuming observer. These conditions also tended to encourage excessive and mindless (growth and) risk-taking, especially with a short-term orientation. Unfortunately, this is true of the growth that led to the 2007/8 U.S. subprime crisis, as well as the 2010 AP microfinance crisis.

Lesson #5: Mere disclosure is not transparency: While transparency (in some cases) did exist in terms of disclosure, several institutions couched the main characteristics of their performance-related remuneration programs in verbose technical language and thereby made it difficult to comprehend for the normal reader. In fact, it was very difficult to get comprehensive information on (a) The total cost of the remuneration program to the institution; (b) The specific performance criteria and measures along with their conceptual and operational definitions; and (c) The manner in which remuneration had been adjusted for relevant risks, especially medium and long-term risks (which is so relevant today). That, from a shareholder's perspective, was *not* ideal by any means! Again, this was the case with the 2007/8 U.S. subprime crisis as also the 2010 AP microfinance crisis.

Without question, FIs will surely need to have remuneration and incentive systems that focus on and encourage at least the medium-term, if not long-term, performance. This, in turn, means that FIs must choose to reward their senior management after significant actual performance has been realized. This has not usually been the case—there are several examples of high, front-loaded one-time bonuses paid to senior management executives of large FIs and the results are there for everyone to see. In fact, in both the financial firms that caused the U.S. subprime (2007/8), as well as Indian MFIs that were behind the Indian microfinance crisis in AP (2010), the focus was on short-term performance, incentives, and compensation—much to the detriment of operations. This certainly needs to be changed to reflect the medium and/or long-term performance and operations.

Also, remuneration at many of these institutions does *not* seem to have been established through an explicit governance process where the roles and responsibilities of all stakeholders involved, including committee members, consultants, risk managers and others, were clearly defined and separated (without conflicts of interest). The roles given to non-executive independent board members in the process—although they may seem somewhat appropriate—again appear to be laden with serious conflicts of interest. And finally, while remuneration policies are sometimes submitted to the annual meeting and subjected to shareholder approval, much of this seems to be a routine matter, with minimal (informed) discussion because of aspects mentioned earlier.

Thus, given this situation, we, as stakeholders, need to continually ask a key question: 'Whether the compensation approaches being pursued are indeed consistent with the FIs' ethics of creating value for clients and its objectives, strategy and control environment as well as that of the overall financial inclusion industry.' And we certainly need to keep looking for objective answers as well.

Therefore, as has been often mentioned, "Compensation is one factor among many that contributed to the financial crisis that began in 2007. Official action to address unsound compensation systems must therefore be embedded in the broader financial regulatory reform programme, built around a substantially stronger and more resilient capital and liquidity framework. Action must be speedy, determined, and coherent. Urgency is particularly important to prevent a return to the compensation practices that contributed to the crisis."[3]

I hope that the various stakeholders focus on this aspect and ensure that the same compensation practices and incentives that (adversely) affected the U.S. subprime and Indian microfinance do not negatively impact the financial inclusion industry (at least, in the future).

Accordingly, I suggest four strategies that these stakeholders should seek to have implemented at FIs in the financial inclusion industry. These practical strategies will ensure that processes in the governance of compensation at FIs become transparent and are indeed perceived to be fair.

Strategy # 1: Enable boards to play a proactive role in the governance of compensation at FIs and prevent the compensation system from being in the grip of the CEO/senior management. First, the boards of FIs can and must play a proactive role in establishing proper governance of remuneration and that is where the buck actually stops. It naturally follows that the board must also ensure that this compensation system is not primarily controlled by the chief executive officer and/or other

---

[3] Quoted from the BIS paper on 'Compensation and Corporate Governance', 2010.

members of the senior management team (CEO, CFO, etc.).

In fact, this has been a major problem with some FIs in the financial inclusion industry. In cases where *the compensation system has tended to be firmly in the grip of the CEO and/or senior management team, it seems prone to nontransparent actions, related-party transactions, and whimsical payouts to CEO/senior management, without sufficient rationale or justification.* In fact, I see this as a major cause for the U.S. subprime (2007/8) as well as the 2010 Indian microfinance crisis in AP—as at these FIs, the compensation decisions were laden with significant conflicts of interest and questionable from a legal as well as ethical standpoint.

Therefore, the concerned stakeholders must ask relevant questions as part of their day-to-day work and ensure course corrections in real time.

- Is the board of directors effectively taking overall responsibility for the FI compensation system, including participating directly in the design and operation of this system?
- Has the board ensured that the CEO and/or senior management team at the MFI are not controlling the compensation system?
- Is the compensation policy aligned with the risk management framework of the MFI?
- Has the board of directors at the FI approved and periodically reviewed the compensation policy?

- Has the board ensured that the compensation policy at the FI does not provide incentives for excessive risk taking and that it is also aligned with medium/long term operations?

Strategy # 2: Ensure that the boards of MFIs have members with requisite compensation experience and real independence, so that they can effectively participate in the regulation of compensation. It is crucial for the FI to have board members with relevant expertise in compensation and perhaps risk management. More importantly, these members must have complete independence in dealing with the (design and operation) of the compensation system. In a way, this is the fulcrum of a fair compensation system where the board members not only have the requisite experience but are also able to use it in an independent and objective manner. This, in turn, implies that the boards of MFIs should not be filled with friends, relatives, and yes-men, as M Damodaran, the former SEBI chairman, has argued.

Again, as evident from the U.S. subprime (2007/8) and the 2010 Indian microfinance crisis in AP, in a few cases, nominee directors and other independent directors seem to have been silenced and their independence compromised (on several occasions) with regard to matters of compensation and remuneration. This again has left a very poor impression of the microfinance industry in India in the minds of the general public.

Here are some key questions in this regard for concerned stakeholders:

- Is the board composed of independent, nonexecutive members, without any conflict of interest?
- Does the board have sufficient expertise (in terms of members) to assess risk management issues related to compensation?
- Does the board have (members with) the skill and experience to reach an independent judgment on the compensation policy?
- Are the relatives of the CEO and/or senior management on the board of the FI? Are there close former associates and/or friends of the CEO/senior management, who are on the board of the FI?
- Can the appointment of these members to the board of the FI be justified in terms of their professional expertise? Or are these relatives/former associates/friends on the board primarily because of their (personal) relationship with the CEO/senior management?

Strategy # 3: Mandate the establishment of an independent board remuneration committee at each FI to oversee the design and implementation of the compensation system. While the previous two strategies articulated the role and responsibility of the board of directors, the key question that arises is how best the boards of FIs can accomplish this in real time. All members of the board cannot spend their entire time on this, nor can individual members of the board work on this in an ad hoc manner.

In other words, there is a critical "how to" with regard to the discharge of the above roles and responsibilities by the FI board—that is, through the establishment of an appropriate independent remuneration committee[4] and defining its mandate. It is through such a committee that the board of directors can design, monitor, and review[5] the compensation system to ensure that it operates as intended. Therefore, it is critical that FIs have a board remuneration committee as an integral part of their governance structure and organization, to oversee the compensation system's design and operation on behalf of the board of directors.

- The remuneration committee should be constituted in a way that enables it to exercise competent and independent judgment[6] on compensation policies/practices and the incentives created (at the FI) for managing risk, capital, liquidity, and customer satisfaction.

---

[4] Sometimes the board may have people with requisite skills and experience and also independence. They, however, need to be appointed to the MFI compensation committee and there are cases, where this has not happened, as the CEO/senior management have desired otherwise.

[5] Two issues are relevant here. One is that the compensation system will need to have controls to ensure compliance and, in some ways, the committee itself is the main control available. Thus, the committee will have to also review the practical operation of the compensation system regularly for compliance with design policies and procedures. Compensation outcomes, risk measurements, and risk outcomes should also be regularly reviewed for consistency on intentions.

[6] BIS paper on 'Compensation and Corporate Governance', 2010.

- In addition, the committee should carefully evaluate the practices by which compensation is paid for potential future revenues, whose timing and likelihood remain uncertain. This is a critical lesson from the 2007/8 U.S. subprime crisis and the 2010 microfinance crisis in AP. While doing so, the committee should demonstrate that its decisions are consistent with an assessment of the FI's true financial condition and future prospects, including medium- and long-term risks.
- To this end, the remuneration committee must work closely with the FI's risk committee in the evaluation of the incentives created by the compensation system.
- It should also ensure that the FI's compensation policy is in compliance with global good practices and standards as well as the respective rules of the national regulatory authorities.

Here are some relevant questions for the concerned stakeholders in this regard.

- Are there controls in place to regularly oversee the compliance of the compensation system? What are these and how sufficient are these controls? Is the independent board remuneration committee one of the key controls?
- In order that the FI board remuneration committee is able to operate independently of the senior executives, is it composed (at a minimum) of a majority of independent, nonexecutive

(board) members without any conflict of interest[7]?

- Does the FI board remuneration committee have (members with) the skill and experience to reach an independent judgment on the compensation policy?
- Do the terms of reference/charter of the board remuneration committee suggest that it has sufficient powers (mandate) to perform its functions independently?
- Is the board remuneration committee at the FI responsible for the preparation of recommendations to the board regarding compensation, including those having implications for risk and risk management?
- Has the board remuneration committee at the FI made recommendations to the board on the compensation to be paid to the highest paid employees, based on a predetermined materiality threshold?
- Does the board remuneration committee at the FI have access to advice, either internal or external, that is independent of advice provided to senior management? What has been the process used for commissioning external advisers to advise the board on compensation policy? Do these advisers report directly to the board remuneration committee?
- Does the board remuneration committee at the FI have unfettered access to information and analysis from risk and control function personnel

---

[7] BIS paper on 'Compensation and Corporate Governance', 2010.

(e.g., risk management, finance, compliance, internal audit, and human resources)?

- Does the board remuneration committee at the FI engage appropriate control function personnel in its deliberations on compensation policy? Do control functions at the FI have input in the structure and determination of compensation?

Strategy # 4: Mandate that MFI board remuneration committees ensure an annual external compensation review. Last but not the least, the remuneration committee should facilitate an annual compensation review at the FI and get it done externally. This review should be independent of any CEO/senior management interference and it should be submitted to the remuneration committee, board of directors, and regulator/supervisor. It should also be disclosed to the public. It goes without saying that this review should, among other things, assess (legal) compliances with the applicable rules and standards promulgated by the relevant regulatory authority. An example from the financial inclusion industry is documented well in *The Economic Times* article by John Samuel Raja D/M Rajshekhar, which notes that Share Microfin's Managing Director's salary was well beyond the limit stipulated by the Companies Act.[8]

---

[8] See 'Share Microfin MD takes home 7.4 crore, more than double HDFC Bank MD's salary' by John Samuel Raja D and M Rajshekhar, *The Economic Times*, February 1, 2011,
https://economictimes.indiatimes.com/jobs/share-microfin-md-takes-home-7-4-cr-more-than-double-hdfc-bank-mds-salary/articleshow/7401434.cms

Some relevant questions in this regard for the concerned stakeholders include the following:
- Is there an external annual compensation review at the FI?
- What is the process for conducting the annual compensation review? Is it an objective and fair process without (any) conflicts of interest?
- Does the annual compensation review assess the compensation policy's compliance with global principles/standards in the microfinance industry, as well as standards (if any) promulgated by the (national) regulators/supervisors?
- Does this include ensuring that all material compensation plans/programs (including those for executives and employees, whose actions have a material impact on the risk exposure of the FI), are covered?
- Does this include assessing the appropriateness of the compensation plans/programs relative to organizational goals, objectives, and risk profile of the FI?

Without question, irrational and ad hoc compensation practices (at some FIs) have been a major factor that appears to have contributed (in significant measure) to the U.S. subprime (2007/8) as well as the 2010 Indian microfinance crisis in AP. Therefore, it is imperative that the various financial services regulators are always on the lookout and take suitable proactive action to address the issue of (such) unsound compensation systems that may crop up from time to time at FIs in the financial inclusion industry. The importance of this task should not be underestimated, as I see this as one of the most important causes leading to these past crisis situations.

Only that can keep future crisis situations at bay and prevent exclusion of the very people we want to financially include in accordance with SDG 1.3.

Chapter 11

Governance of Risk Management Imperative to Prevent Financial Exclusion

Lack of sound corporate governance leads to poor risk management at financial institutions (FIs). Sound corporate governance is critical as it can enhance the quality of risk management, including processes adopted for the same. As governance involves many stakeholders, each with specific assigned responsibilities, they need to ensure that the system as a whole is geared to support the overall strategy of the financial institution and ensure the effectiveness of various internal control mechanisms. Further, while the board is certainly not expected to understand every nuance of the business or to oversee every activity/transaction, they need to ensure that senior management does that using an organized hierarchy of responsibilities with clear authority. The board, however, has the responsibility to set the tone regarding their own financial institution's risk taking (preferences) and to oversee the internal control strategy so as to ensure that their directives are actually followed on the ground, during implementation. They also have the responsibility to hire staff, who, in their opinion, have the integrity, judgment and competence to help achieve the same. This did not happen with either the FIs at the heart of the U.S. subprime crisis (2007/8) or the microfinance institutions (MFIs) at the heart of the 2010 Indian microfinance crisis in Andhra Pradesh (AP). The case of the Indian banking crisis (2018) clearly shows that this did not happen at the concerned financial institution (i.e., Punjab National Bank [PNB]) as well.

In my opinion, one of the most important fallouts of the past crisis situations has been the apparent lack of and/or failure of risk management at many FIs. I have several generic and specific observations regarding this for ministries of finance, central banks and other financial service regulators who are at the forefront of driving the financial inclusion agenda.

- *Internal controls for financial reporting versus risk management:* In many FIs, the (sole) focus on internal controls was mainly for the purpose of financial reporting. This resulted in risk management deviating from strategy and its implementation. Also, in several FIs, the basic tenets of internal control, particularly those pertaining to operating risks, were not followed.

- *Risk handled in a piecemeal manner:* In a few cases, the enterprise (or FI) as a whole was not considered and risk was handled in a piecemeal manner—so much so that even the boards were completely out of touch with the (risk management) systems in place. Thus, a holistic and comprehensive perspective on risk was lacking.
- *Risk management mistaken for risk elimination:* In many FIs, effective risk management was seen as eliminating risk taking and that is perhaps an inappropriate view of things. FIs and other stakeholders must understand that risk is a fundamental driving force in any activity, including financial services and financial inclusion. Therefore, risk elimination is perhaps not strictly possible. The aim must be to ensure that the risks are understood, managed, and, where appropriate, communicated throughout the organization, so that the FI as a whole can be ready for it, as and when it becomes significant.
- *Inability to seriously anticipate and properly manage political[1], regulatory[2] and other risks:* In several FIs, the political risk (as in the Indian microfinance crisis in AP in 2010) was neither (seriously)

---

[1] This is in spite of dress rehearsals such as the Krishna (2005–2006) microfinance crisis and Kolar 2009 microfinance crisis having occurred in India.

[2] An example of regulatory risk is the case of 'Bandhan Bank', which, post listing, received a notice in September 2018 from the RBI placing certain restrictions on the opening of new branches. This led to the plummeting of Bandhan Bank's share value on October 1, 2018. The share value fell to Rs 452.20—down 20% (or by a whopping Rs 113.05) in a single day—adversely impacting its retail and institutional investors as also other stakeholders.

anticipated nor managed on an institution-wide basis. Those (initially) looking at this risk were perhaps either far too junior or lacked the requisite contextual experience; often, there seemed to be no serious guidance from the senior management/board. Importantly, the boards were, in a number of cases, ignorant of the key (political and important) risks facing their FIs, and most came into the picture later than required.

- *Lack of board involvement in establishing/overseeing risk management structure:* Without question, the effective implementation of risk management requires involving the board in both establishing and overseeing the risk management structure. This did not happen and, in many FIs, the board neither reviewed nor provided guidance about the alignment of overall strategy with risk appetite and the internal risk management structure.

- *Lack of independence of risk management and control functions:* To assist the board in its work, risk management and control functions need to be independent, reporting directly to the board. However, this was seldom the case, and, as a result, risk perceptions often got altered (or even misreported) by the line management and other staff. In reality, such risk perceptions were perhaps not fair representations of the true risk confronting the FI (*a situation akin to not wanting any bad news, often without realizing that timely news about things going wrong affords a greater chance to undertake appropriate on-course corrections*). Thus, a true picture of the risks perhaps never reached the board, which was left high and dry when the same affected the FI.

That said, how then can the governance of risk management be improved in FIs? But before getting into the recommendations, let us ask a relevant question here: *Why have these risk management failures occurred and what are the lessons for financial inclusion?*

The answer is simple. *FIs that have faced burgeoning growth in the past few years have not had commensurate capacity—including internal control and other systems—required for managing their turbocharged growth.* Furthermore, as a result of their burgeoning growth, many of these FIs are increasingly vulnerable to fraud and control failures (especially when their growth shears and stresses their systems). We need to learn from these internal control lapses and these lessons must be dovetailed into the financial inclusion paradigm.

Issue # 1: Lack of sound corporate governance leads to poor risk management at the FIs. Sound corporate governance is critical as it can enhance the quality of risk management, including the processes adopted for the same at an FI. As governance involves many stakeholders, each with specific assigned responsibilities, they need to ensure that the system as a whole is geared to support the overall strategy of the FI and ensure the effectiveness of various internal control mechanisms. Furthermore, while the board is certainly not expected to understand every nuance of the microfinance business and/or to oversee every microfinance activity/transaction, they need to ensure that senior management does that using an organized hierarchy of responsibilities with clear authority. The board, however, has the responsibility of setting the tone regarding their own FIs' risk taking (preferences) and to oversee the internal control strategy so as to ensure that their directives are actually followed on the ground, during implementation. They also have the responsibility to hire staff, who, in their opinion, have the integrity, judgment, and competence to help achieve the same. This, unfortunately, did not happen with the FIs at the heart of the past crisis situations—be it the U.S. subprime (2007/8), or the Indian microfinance crisis in AP (2010) or the Indian banking crisis (PNB-2018).

Issue # 2: Disregard for internal controls by many line managers. Internal controls are the responsibility of line management at MFIs. Line managers must determine the level of risks they need to accept to run their businesses and to assure that the combination of earnings, capital, and internal controls is sufficient to compensate for the risk exposures. *It is clear from the past crisis situations that the basic tenets of 'internal control', particularly those pertaining to operating and related risks, were not followed*—in fact, as the analysis of many (fraud) cases demonstrate, it is apparent that the line managers in several fast growing FIs had utter disregard for even the most basic controls, such as the segregation of duties, and so on.

Issue # 3: Enhanced people risks also causing failure of internal controls. Internal controls and sound governance become more important when the FIs' operations move into higher risk areas—such as the kind of growth that many of the FIs experienced prior to the 2007/8 (U.S. subprime) or 2010 (Indian microfinance) crisis. Indeed, when changes are happening, as they had been during these high growth periods, there is no doubt that control failures will increase significantly, as has been reported. Thus, rapid growth, the introduction of new products and processes, and changes in delivery channels are examples of situations that stress the FI control environment. When these types of changes occur, 'people risks'—risks that are related to training employees in new products and processes—escalate. Employees who join will undoubtedly need to learn about the culture and control environment at the FI. Likewise, employees unfamiliar with their new responsibilities, including the systems they use, their changing client profile, the services they provide customers, the degree of attention expected by their own supervisors (and members of the internal control department), are more likely to create control breaks. As a result, FIs need to be wary of and manage people risks appropriately and in a timely manner, through good human resources function. This again has been and continues to be very weak at most FIs—especially those pushing the frontiers of the financial inclusion industry.

Issue # 4: Drive for efficiency causing omission of key controls. Rapid growth and change also modify the relative risks to an FI. For example, the pressure to beat a competitor in the market with new/same products (as was the case in the U.S. or in AP during the years preceding the various crisis situations) may cut short the design review process and omit an important aspect of control. This has happened consistently and the drive for efficiency and use of more standardized processes also led to very little time being invested in building client-level relationships, which incidentally was the key and hallmark feature in the early success of many FIs.

Issue # 5: Entrepreneurial drive and nontransparent governance results in lack of control infrastructure. In fact, many of the FIs that had been at the center of the U.S. subprime (2007/8) or the Indian microfinance crisis in AP (2010) came under the microscope for their governance failures and they demonstrated similar characteristics. They were led by hard-charging entrepreneurs/CEOs whose ability to think outside the box (in all fairness) pioneered growth, advances and innovation. *But the personalities of these individuals, in many cases, led to a single-minded focus on unmanageable growth, higher profits, increased equity investments, share valuations at a premium, higher returns and larger 'wealth creation' for shareholders. This perhaps resulted in very little time being spent on building the control infrastructure so vital for the delivery of financial services.* In fact, as a result of this, inadequate time was spent on building the control infrastructure, unequal to the amount required in such an environment. The consequences are there for all to see.

Issue # 6: Irrational expectations and internal frauds. Another form of risk is internal fraud. When the expectations of the market, supervisors, and colleagues, or pressures of professional/personal life become overwhelming, key FI staff may overstep ethical and legal boundaries and cover up errors or deliberately commit a fraud. *This is what has happened in many FIs (in these past crisis situations) that turbocharged themselves to grow at any cost.* There is enough reason to believe that this may have been the case with several of the staff at these FIs who were found to be involved in frauds (before and during the crisis situations). Again, the human resources function must take the driver's seat and reduce (or, if possible, eliminate) unrealistic expectations and ease work time pressures, so that the FI staff are not forced to cross the line, with regard to ethical behavior on the job. An important aspect is to ensure that there should be no disconnect between strategy and risk management, on the one hand, and incentives on the other. Incentives do not just mean remuneration but also other aspects such as promotion, stock options, and so on. That would help in reducing 'people risks'.

Issue # 7: Weakened internal audit function in many FIs. Boards of directors at FIs are responsible for ensuring that their FIs have an effective audit process and that internal controls are adequate for the nature and scope of their businesses. The reporting lines of the internal audit function should be such that the information directors receive is impartial and not unduly influenced by management. Internal audit is a key element of the overall responsibility to validate the strength of internal controls. This is not to be underestimated. *This sadly did not happen in many FIs and, especially, in the larger FIs. The same weakness can be found in many large and fast growing FIs.*

Issue # 8: Greater focus on quantitative versus qualitative risks. Thus, although risk management has become more quantitative, considerable management judgment must be applied to the process, and this is what FIs need to get their boards to facilitate. Frequent and small losses can generally be absorbed in the operating margin of the product or service and FIs have tended to focus more on such risks and problems. It is the low-probability, large losses that provide the greatest challenge. It is just such risks—the ones that can severely damage, if not kill, an organization—that too many FIs have not formally taken into consideration. And that, in many ways, has resulted in many problems on the ground in these past crisis situations.

I would like to mention that as the financial inclusion industry moves forward, risk assessment and risk-based auditing[3] at systemically important and large FIs becomes necessary. I do hope that all FIs—including fast growing, large and new age (FinTech) ones—adopt this and the regulatory framework makes it necessary for them to do so. This alone can help prevent the kind of institutional lapses that led to the either the U.S. subprime (2007/8) or the

---

[3] In simple terms, risk assessment is a process by which an auditor identifies and evaluates the quantity of the FI's risks and the quality of its controls over those risks. Through risk-based auditing, the board and auditors will use the results of the risk assessments to focus on the areas of greatest risk and to set priorities for audit work. That, however, does not mean that the audit department can lose sight of or ignore areas that are rated low risk. An effective risk-based auditing program will ensure adequate audit coverage for all of an FI's auditable activities. The frequency and depth of each area's audit should vary according to the auditor's risk assessment.

Indian microfinance crises in AP (2010)—both of which led to the exclusion of large numbers of people whom we were trying to include in the first place.

I sincerely hope that the financial inclusion industry looks at these and other issues related to internal controls arising from the past crisis situations. That is one area, among many others, where rebuilding can and must start as soon as possible. Only this can put the financial inclusion industry on a firm footing and get it to implement—through a sound independent internal audit function[4]—the great-sounding ideas that FIs always wanted to implement so as to ensure 100% sustained financial inclusion.

---

[4] Independent internal audits, which are equally important, are dealt with in chapter 12.

Chapter 12

Independent Internal Audits, the Key to Responsible Financial Inclusion Services

Why is an independent and objective internal audit system critical for the well-being of financial institutions[1] (FIs), especially those desiring to practice responsible financial inclusion services (RFIS)? From a larger perspective, internal audits are perhaps the first means for well-meaning FI boards to get regular feedback on whether or not the concept of responsible FI is being implemented on the ground. In other words, an independent and objective internal audit system can provide very useful feedback on how processes and procedures (to

---

[1] The term FI is used denote a wide variety of organizations including commercial and other banks, nonbanking financial institutions, cooperatives and credit unions, other forms of microfinance institutions, FinTech firms and so on.

promote responsible FI) are supposedly being implemented on the ground. And it is the internal audit system that can provide very useful early warning signals for the FIs and their boards. Without question, just as charity begins at home, the first step in RFIS is therefore to ensure that FIs have an independent and objective internal audit system in the first place.

So, what do I mean by an independent and objective internal audit system? I will start out here by setting the strategic context of internal audits from which their independence and objectivity stem. This strategic context clearly determines the extent to which internal audits can become a powerful and independent tool that boards of FIs can use to ensure RFIS on the ground and in real time.

Essentially, according to The Institute of Internal Auditors, internal auditing is defined as: *"An independent, objective assurance... activity designed to add value and improve an organization's operations. It helps an organization accomplish its objectives by bringing a systematic, disciplined approach to evaluate and improve the effectiveness of risk management, control, and governance processes."*[2] The above definition is critical because it sets forth the parameters on which an internal audit system can be designed at the FIs.

First and foremost, *an internal audit system must be independent of the FI activities being audited.* This implies

---

[2] See 'About Internal Auditing', *The Institute of Internal Auditors*, https://global.theiia.org/about/about-internal-auditing/Pages/About-Internal-Auditing.aspx

that internal auditors at FIs don't report to line management and/or senior management. Often, at some FIs which had an elaborate internal audit function, the independence of this function was hugely compromised because the internal audit department came under senior management, whose very activities were also to be assessed.

Tell me, how can an internal audit department that reports to the CEO or CFO (or anyone else who is part of the line/operational management) accurately assess and provide objective feedback on the workings of processes and procedures[3]? *Therefore, the FI boards must ensure that there is an internal audit department that reports directly to the board or its audit sub-committee.* This is mandatory and this independence in functioning will facilitate greater objectivity in the working of the internal audit department. It will also position the internal audit department appropriately within the FI.

Second, an additional caveat is in order here. Many organizations, including FIs, may find it tempting to get internal auditors to design their risk management, control and governance systems. While it is true that internal auditors have intimate knowledge of what systems work on the ground and why, if they are asked to design these FI systems, then, it is unlikely

---

[3] Past crisis situations—be it the U.S. subprime (2007/8) or 2010 Indian microfinance crisis in Andhra Pradesh or the 2018 Indian banking crisis like PNB—clearly suggest that internal auditors, because they lacked independence and objectivity, failed in their duty on the job, which indeed proved to be a key cause for these crisis situations in the first place.

that they would be able to assess functioning of these systems dispassionately and objectively. *This means that, at no time, should FIs use their internal auditors to design the risk management, control and governance systems and processes.* At best, feedback—through discussions with the internal auditors and/or studying of their internal audit reports—could be taken with regard to these systems so that appropriate on-course corrections are made. This again will ensure that the internal auditors are truly independent of the activities that they are auditing.

A third issue is relevant here. That is, the scope of internal audits, and this again is critical to understanding the reality from across the organization (or FI). Very often, the activities of senior management are excluded from internal audits for various reasons. That should not be the case. In short, internal audits must cover each and every activity at the FI with the objective of evaluating (but not limited to) the following:

- Integrity, reliability and effectiveness (including the relevance, accuracy and comprehensiveness) of risk management, control and governance processes and related systems;
- Monitoring of legal compliances—with extant laws and regulations—including any changing requirements from regulator/supervisors; and
- Safeguarding of all assets of the FI.

Without question, the need for strong, independent and objective internal audits has never been more important in the financial service sector. I certainly hope that the boards (in FIs) recognize this and facilitate the adoption of well-functioning internal audit systems that can go a long way in *protecting their FIs and enhancing their reputation as real practitioners of RFIS globally.*

Having stressed the importance of the independence of internal audits, the next question to ask is how to design the internal audit function at FIs?

First of all, let us get the facts straight. Internal auditors play a critical role in any FI. The primary role of internal auditors is to independently and objectively review and evaluate an FI's activities to maintain or improve the efficiency and effectiveness of risk management, internal controls, and corporate governance. As noted above, they do this by:

- Evaluating the reliability, adequacy, and effectiveness of accounting, operating, and administrative controls.
- Ensuring that FI internal controls result in prompt and accurate recording of transactions and proper safeguarding of assets.
- Determining whether an FI complies with laws and regulations and adheres to established policies.
- Determining whether management is taking the appropriate steps to address current and prior control deficiencies and audit report recommendations.

For this, internal auditors must understand an FI's strategic direction, objectives, products, services, and processes, as well as clients, to conduct these activities and make an objective judgment on the above. The auditors then communicate their findings to the board of directors or its audit committee, who then will brief and discuss with senior management.

In addition, internal auditors often have a role in transformation activities. This role may include duties such as helping the board and management evaluate safeguards and controls, including appropriate documentation and audit trails, during the transformation process at the FI—this is a critical issue as many FIs transform, in some sense or another, to keep up with the highly dynamic nature of the financial inclusion and financial services industry.

While the point that FIs should conduct their internal audit activities according to existing professional standards and guidance is well taken, how exactly the internal audit function is accomplished depends on the FI's size, complexity, scope of activities, and risk profile, as well as the responsibilities assigned to the internal auditor by the board of directors.

In larger FIs, a chief auditor and a full-time internal audit staff may accomplish the internal audit function. In other FIs, the internal audit function may be accomplished by one or two employees or a holding company or even by an outside vendor. In many small FIs, the officer or employee designated as a part-time auditor may also have operational responsibilities. In any case, to maintain independence, the person responsible for accomplishing the internal audit function should be independent of whatever area is being audited and should report their findings directly to the board and/or its audit committee.

The audit committee should position the internal audit function in the institution's organizational structure so that the function will perform its duties with impartiality and not be unduly influenced by managers of day-to-day operations. The ideal organizational arrangement is having the internal audit function report directly and solely to the audit committee regarding both internal audit issues and administrative matters, e.g., resources, budget, and compensation.

Some FIs place the manager of internal audit under a dual reporting arrangement: *functionally accountable to the audit committee for matters such as the design of audit plans and the review of audit scope and audit findings, while reporting to a senior executive on administrative matters.* Such an arrangement potentially limits the internal audit manager's independence and objectivity when auditing the senior executive's lines of business.

Thus, the chief financial officer, controller, or other similar positions should generally be excluded from overseeing the internal audit activities even in a dual role. In structuring the reporting hierarchy, the audit committee should weigh this risk of diminished independence against the benefit of reduced administrative burden in adopting a dual reporting organizational structure.

Without a doubt, the best option of course is to ensure that the internal audit departmental head reports directly to the board or audit committee of the FI, to ensure that all potential and real conflicts of interests are negated. *In reality, the board should be and is responsible for delegating the authority necessary to effectively allow internal auditors to perform their job. Thus, internal auditors must have the power to act on their own initiative in all departments, functions and units in the FI; to communicate directly with any FI personnel; and to gain access to all records, files, or data necessary for the proper conduct of the audit.* Clear communication between the board, the internal auditors, and management is critical to the timely identification and correction of weaknesses in internal controls and operations.

To summarize, internal auditors play a very fundamental role in ensuring the integrity of the various systems at FIs and, therefore, it is important that they are given the necessary authority, independence and skills/knowledge to effectively perform their crucial tasks. And unless this happens, neither the financial inclusion industry nor the financial services sector will be capable of truly achieving the dream of protecting customers[4] and ensuring 100% sustained financial inclusion on the ground by 2030, in accordance with SDG 1.3.

---

[4] See chapter 13 for aspects related to customer protection.

Chapter 13

Customer Protection, the Key to Sustained Financial Inclusion

Financial inclusion and digital financial inclusion are the new buzzwords in the financial sector industry. Indeed there has been a lot of innovation in the area of financial inclusion and digital financial inclusion and the number of products on offer. The stakeholders who have delivered these products have increased significantly as well—both of which have contributed to immensely enhancing the complexity of financial inclusion and digital financial inclusion products and services. So, it naturally follows that protection of the end user clients—of financial inclusion and digital financial inclusion products and services—becomes very necessary. There can be no two doubts about that!

Powering A Billion Dreams

Now, if you look at financial inclusion, traditionally the suppliers of these products and services have been banks, nonbanking financial institutions, cooperatives, credit unions, microfinance institutions[1] and other institutions, some of which are regulated and supervised, and others are not. Thus, while some of these institutions come under the purview of the central bank, others do not. However, when digital financial inclusion services come into play, service providers typically include FinTech start-ups,[2] TELCOS[3] and a whole range of merchants, agents and intermediaries. Technically, while these stakeholders come under the central bank regulations (in their respective countries of operation), their supervision is most certainly not as it should be, especially from a client protection perspective. Therefore, for both financial inclusion and digital financial inclusion services, it would be appropriate to argue that, at best, client protection services and client redressal mechanisms are in their infancy.

This is because if you look at central banks (like the Reserve Bank in India), especially in large, diverse countries like India, even for the few institutions that they regulate and supervise, they don't have the wherewithal to provide dispersed, decentralized and grass-roots level client redressal mechanisms and client protection services, which are very much required for low-income and bottom of pyramid

---

[1] Examples include: Trusts, Societies, Shuras etc.
[2] FinTech uses technology to deliver financial services. FinTech companies are typically startups and they are disruptive innovations.
[3] Telecommunications companies are called TELCOS.

(BoP) clients. And the mere delegation of supervision and client protection issues to self-regulatory organizations (SROs) does not and will not work, as self-regulation is an oxy-moron.

Member-controlled SROs cannot self-regulate and we have had innumerable examples over the last 13 years from across the globe, since the Indian microfinance crisis of 2005/6 in Krishna district of Andhra Pradesh (AP). Some other prominent examples include the U.S. subprime of 2007/8 and the Indian microfinance crisis of 2010 in AP, whose various fallouts have been thoroughly discussed in chapters two and three.

That being the case, the only feasible option is for clients to approach the banking ombudsman and use other existing mechanisms traditionally available in the traditional financial sector. However, the transactions costs associated with going to a banking ombudsman (and/or similar traditional mechanisms) can indeed be huge and prohibitive for low-income and BoP clients, who tend to get intimidated by the very nature of these highly bureaucratic systems. I am saying this with strong conviction because even somebody like me, who is educated and 'tech savvy' and belongs to what we call the middle class (in an economic sense in India), found it difficult to approach the banking ombudsman. Believe me when I say, it is indeed extremely difficult to reach the banking ombudsman. I did try some years ago and in fact, I needed all kinds of references before I could even get an official appointment with the banking ombudsman in my area! So, not to sound like a broken record, but low income and BoP clients will almost find it impossible to reach the banking ombudsman (and/or similar mechanisms)—let us be absolutely clear on that aspect.

And then of course you may have other frameworks that attempt to protect the end-user customers—this could typically include customer protection acts and/or competition acts in the respective countries. Again, it is my experience that low income and excluded clients find it extremely difficult to even get access to agencies under these acts because the agencies tend to be very bureaucratic and highly formal. When access itself is difficult, the question of getting justice becomes even more remote. In fact, accessing these is very difficult, even for a person like me. I am therefore certain that low-income and BoP clients will find it extremely cumbersome to access these bodies and avail of their services. Thus, the larger point that I am trying to make is, low-income and/or BoP clients face huge difficulty in accessing the currently available client redressal mechanisms, whether be it the banking ombudsman scheme and/or other alternatives that presently exist.

The sum and substance of my argument is that low-income and/or BoP clients face huge hurdles in reaching out to the people who possess the executive powers to take action against those financial inclusion and digital financial inclusion stakeholders, who may have violated consumer protection norms and guidelines in the first place.

Another aspect that has to be kept in mind is that in

many countries, legislative enactment and framing of rules and regulations is easily done, but when it comes to the actual implementation of laws and regulations and rules in real time, the record is rather poor. And the implementation of laws and regulations and rules gets poorer and weaker the more distant and remote the place is—so, when you are talking of remote places which are now experiencing burgeoning growth of (digital) financial inclusion services and where huge violations of clients' rights are taking place, the question that arises is, "How do clients living in these areas protect themselves and how can they access client redressal mechanisms easily and quickly?"

As it stands, the truth of the matter is that it is going to be very difficult for the central bank or, for that matter, any mainstream financial service regulator, to even know of the client protection violations that are happening on the ground. And unless they are aware that violations are occurring and the specific nature of these violations, they will not be able to regulate, because I think the ability of low-income or BoP clients to bring client protection issues back to the regulator (sitting in a faraway place) is almost next to impossible. And there is, of course, the issue of intimidation that these low-income and BoP clients face for various reasons, because of which they are less likely to approach a regulator located far away.

So I think the case for having an independent client protection regulator (with a deeply entrenched grass-roots network) becomes very strong. With all due respect, I think that central banks and other financial service regulators should regulate financial institutions with regard to prudential and non-prudential norms and also look at institutional and organizational issues and other aspects. However, when it comes to the issue of client protection, a highly specialized body will have to take charge of that.

Thus, client protection requires a new country level independent agency (regulator) with a strong grass-roots presence. And it must be an agency which is neither involved in the development of (digital) financial inclusion and microfinance services nor concerned with regulating other aspects of these (digital) financial inclusion and microfinance stakeholders. In other words, this client protection agency (regulator) should have a single-minded focus on customer protection and look at everything from the perspective of the end-user clients with regard to (digital) financial inclusion and microfinance. Single-minded focus is required and only then will this regulator be able to do justice and ensure client protection at the grass roots, which has far-ranging and far-reaching consequences for the (digital) financial inclusion and microfinance industry in the long term!

The rationale for an independent agency becomes more important when you look at the following context. People have often asked me why the regulation and supervision of microfinance and (digital) financial inclusion and, especially, protection of end-user clients has generally been weak in many countries globally. I attribute this to the following reasons.

First is the near seamless shift of key people from the private financial sector to regulatory and supervisory bodies through the *reverse revolving door* phenomenon. I have known top executives of large financial conglomerates (interested in financial inclusion and microfinance) and representatives of special interest groups including lobbyists, who have built up close (working) relationships with the regulators and supervisors—in particular those who oversee or regulate the financial inclusion and microfinance sector.

Specifically, these key people from the private financial sector, with a deep interest in financial inclusion and microfinance, have then been appointed to the governing boards, expert committees and/or senior management at regulatory and supervisory bodies (whose mandate also includes the regulation and supervision of the financial inclusion and microfinance sector).

The reverse revolving door phenomenon is characterized by people establishing a very strong pro-financial inclusion and microfinance bias in policy formulation and regulatory enforcement by regulators and supervisors that oversee their (former) industry, former employers and/or related institutions. When I talk of regulatory enforcement, I am talking about end-user client protection issues in particular, which have not got the kind of attention that they require and deserve, especially given what happened in the Indian microfinance crisis in Andhra Pradesh (2010) or U.S. subprime (2007/8).

And given the huge end-user client protection and other risks that are prevalent in (digital) financial inclusion and microfinance products and delivery processes, I am simply amazed at the above happening.

Second, I have seen the shift of key people from government institutions to the private (financial inclusion and microfinance) sector through the *normal revolving door phenomenon.* I am talking of the case where key people from regulatory and supervisory bodies, development finance institutions (DFIs) and other government lenders and institutions have moved (either through a permanent and/or temporary relationship) to lucrative private sector positions (in financial inclusion and microfinance). Again, irrespective of whatever happens, end-user client protection cannot and must not suffer, but that is what is happening in real time (sadly)!

And interestingly, these people use their regulatory and government experience and long-standing connections to benefit their new employer and/or industry directly as well as indirectly (e.g., through the drafting of a supportive regulatory policy, in public procurement, and so on and so forth). This has not only led to a lax regulatory environment and poor supervision by their former colleagues (with regard to the financial inclusion and microfinance sector) but has also resulted in the drafting and framing of policies hugely supportive to the financial inclusion and microfinance industry, especially at the expense of end-user client protection and well-being. Again, this is not at all acceptable under any circumstance!

While I can easily name people and institutions, my objective is not that but rather to isolate the generic reasons for lack of improvement in the regulatory and supervisory environment for (digital) financial inclusion and microfinance, especially with regard to end-user client protection.

Third, I have also seen situations where former decision makers (including policy makers and executive decision makers) have become *paid advocates* and used their knowledge of and connections with governmental agencies and regulators and supervisors to advance the interests of (corporate) microfinance and financial inclusion companies.

These paid advocates are involved in lobbying a generalist view on the public good[4] nature of financial inclusion and microfinance services, when in fact there is much harassment of end-user clients that is taking place at the grass roots and a whole lot of money is being made illegally (especially at the local level) at the expense of low-income and BoP clients. The agents who rule at the grass roots make it very expensive—whether monetarily and/or physically for low-income and BoP clients. Why are the regulators and supervisors turning a blind eye? Do not the end-user clients matter in the large scheme of things? These and other questions

---

[4] The term is used as in common parlance—See the following for an explanation of the same, https://en.wikipedia.org/wiki/Public_good

continue to run through my mind, even as I write this book!

The larger point that I want to make from all of this is that the grass roots reality is very different from what is being portrayed, and there is hardly any regulation and supervision and client protection that is going on in real time (especially at the grass roots)! And I am not talking of interest rates here but the fact that a whole lot of money is being made at the grass roots (in the financial inclusion and microfinance sector) through mechanisms that are illegal, unethical and client unfriendly. And it is my humble belief that this calls for a serious effort to create a *truly independent end user client protection regulator* for (digital) financial inclusion and microfinance with a strong grass-roots presence and executive powers so that end-user client protection indeed becomes a reality and can be ensured in real time always!

Indeed, if you look at the structure of what's happening in digital financial inclusion, you will see a large number of stakeholders getting involved, and these are not necessarily financial institutions. TELCOS, merchants, intermediaries, agents and a whole range of other new stakeholders, including FinTech startups, are getting involved in the delivery of (digital) financial inclusion services. That is fine but what is very important and also needs to be noted is that none of them have serious regulatory and supervisory oversight and because of that clients' rights are being violated!

Let me give a few examples of what happened to a friend to illustrate what I am saying. This friend recently started using a digital wallet (through his mobile) to top up air time and also buy small things. On several occasions, his complaint was that due to poor network connectivity and/or some other (technical) reason, the money had been debited from his digital wallet account but the purchase did not go through. He claimed that this is also happened in the case of his recently acquired credit card, and he offers these two instances.

First, when he tried to top up his mobile, a transaction for **Rs** 500 (about U.S. $ 7.50) through his digital wallet, the money got debited from his digital wallet account but then the TELCO did not top up the air time. He called their customer care department (with great difficulty as there was a long list of options to go through and choose from to reach the customer service staff) and the staff were extremely rude. When he told them about the problem, they said they would check and revert and, soon enough, he got a message from the TELCO saying that, due to technical reasons, the top up did not happen. It is important to note that he did not get any message initially but got this only after he spoke to the customer service staff.

He again called their customer care and told them that his money had been debited already, for which the customer service staff said it would take at least 5 working days for the money to appear back in his digital wallet. The key point to note here is that, apart from not getting the air time top up, which my friend

206

required at that point in time, he was also poorer by Rs 500 (about U.S. $ 7.50) for a few days. Technically that was his money and it should not have been parked with someone else—either the digital wallet owner and/or the TELCO to whom it did not belong. In this case, the digital wallet was owned by the TELCO and so the money was essentially with the TELCO.

The flip side is that if several such transactions occurred in a day, imagine the money that the digital wallet company and/or the TELCO would be holding (unfairly). This is one serious issue with (digital) financial inclusion and needs to be noted by the regulators. And when this happens, while the amounts may be small for the individual clients, the aggregated amounts can be large on a country wide basis for the digital wallet company and/or the TELCO.

Second, the friend related a similar happening in the case of an airline booking through his mobile phone using his recently acquired credit card. Now, that's again using a digital financial inclusion service where my friend used his smart credit card through his mobile and the money for the transaction was debited and went into the account of the airline (and/or merchant) but the ticket was not issued.

To summarize, countries which are looking seriously to further financial inclusion services and digital financial services in a big way must immediately create a customer protection agency. I most certainly agree that digital financial services entities, including

FinTech firms, are a great way to bring hitherto excluded people into the financial system. But that cannot happen without due process and one of the key ingredients for the same is the availability of a country-wide customer protection body with a strong grass-roots presence that low-income and excluded clients will be able to easily access.

Right now, with the proliferation of many newer kinds of financial inclusion and digital financial services, consumers have no place to go. Calling the toll free helpline that some of the service providers have is a harrowing experience—it goes into an endless loop and when the customer care executive comes on, they more often than not turn out to be very rude, besides leaving the customer helpless in terms of providing a real solution.

The same goes for banks and one finds bizarre charges in their statements time and again, which the customer care department is not even willing to explain to the affected end users. Thus, millions of customers of financial institutions are being subjected to various forms of exploitative behavior and this ultimately results in their exclusion. While codes of conduct exist on paper, they are rarely followed. And, most importantly, the central bank and other financial service regulators have neither the wherewithal nor time to address these critical customer protection issues.

Therefore, in every country, the need of the hour is a customer protection body that can:

1. Deter misconduct by enforcing the rules,
2. Discipline those who break the rules,
3. Detect and prevent wrongdoing in financial markets,
4. Educate and inform customers,
5. Resolve disputes, where possible,
6. Most importantly, ensure fair products and services are provided to all people so that they can be financially included in a sustained manner, especially in accordance with SDG 1.3, which calls for 100% sustained financial inclusion by 2030

While the Financial Industry Regulatory Authority, Inc. (FINRA,[5] United States) is a great beginning, the same must happen in all other countries of the world—only then can the aspect of 100% sustained financial inclusion by 2030 in accordance with SDG 1.3 become an achievable goal in real time.

And for that to happen, not only should every country have a separate customer protection agency—as articulated in this chapter—that regulates and supervises traditional and new age financial institutions on how they treat their customers (in terms of products, processes and the like) but they must also tighten their regulatory and supervisory framework, using technology,[6] so that early warning signals and quick regulatory responses are available to prevent financial crisis situations that could stall our progress towards 100% sustained financial inclusion by 2030.

---

[5] See https://www.finra.org/
[6] See chapter 14 for use of RegTech in regulation and supervision.

Chapter 14

RegTech, the Key to Proactive Regulation and Supervision

If we go back to chapter three, it becomes very evident that in all the past financial crisis situations, the governments, central banks, regulators and supervisors were extremely ill-prepared for the impending crisis. Of course, while their incoherent responses in great measure added to the uncertainty and panic in the financial markets, a major problem was that early warning signals were either not there or, at best, not discernible.

Also, these were shrouded by conflicts of interest that were at play, in particular because of the seamless exchange of people from the financial services industry to the regulatory domain and vice versa, through what is commonly called as the revolving door and reverse revolving door phenomenon.

In effect, we had what can be called regulatory and supervisory failure coupled with a serious breakdown in accountability and ethics, right from the grassroots level to the corporate boardrooms, and regulators and supervisors, who sat and watched as Icarus[1] continued to fly high. In turn, this had an impact not just as (disastrous) financial consequences but it also led to a serious erosion of trust in the financial system and all of its constituents, including regulators and supervisors, by the public at large (including customers, depositors, investors, end users and others)—who will all need to stay financially included in a sustained manner if we are to achieve SDG 1.3 by 2030.

Having set the context, we can safely argue that, as compared to the past financial crisis situation (e.g., the U.S. subprime), today's institutions are larger and riskier. Therefore, we cannot simply afford to have regulatory and supervisory failure going forward. Part of the problem is that with the burgeoning growth of institutions and their portfolio, as well as clients, the information coming to the regulators and supervisors is clearly what I would call information overload. And the larger the bulk in compliance reporting, the lesser the chance of spotting exceptions, and the greater the chance of fraud and a full-blown financial crisis—both of which again cause exclusion of

---

[1] See 'Madam President: History in the Making?', Ramesh S Arunachalam, July 2016, published by AuthorsUpFront, New Delhi and https://en.wikipedia.org/wiki/Icarus

people in large measure, as demonstrated by the U.S. subprime (2007/8) and Indian microfinance crisis in Andhra Pradesh (2010).

Therefore, what are required are SMART RegTech tools that will help regulators and supervisors pick up early warning signals about impending crisis situations in the financial services sector, and information on the key aspects that caused the past financial crisis in the first place—things like whether the compensation policy is rewarding the quick deal when the risks are indeed medium or long term, or whether conflicts of interest are causing a financial institution (and other stakeholders) to go rogue, or what the real (hidden) leverage of a financial institution is, after taking into account all aspects such as off balance sheet items, etc.

And that is where the current applications of RegTech for regulation and supervision fall short—they primarily center around KYC (know your customer) and AML (anti-money laundering) and other such compliances and this is akin to skimming the market. To realize the full potential of RegTech (especially machine and deep learning), two crucial things will have to happen.

One, central banks, as well as other regulators and supervisors, will have to remove any ambiguity in rules and circulars to their constituents. The discretionary power of the regulator and supervisor will also have to go so that the rules governing the game are crystal clear and not subject to interpretation and the whims and fancies of the regulator and supervisor.

Two, machine and deep learning, on their part, will have to develop the ability to discern causality (as opposed to mere correlation and association) to have greater predictive ability for regulators and supervisors. And it is the fusion of deep domain knowledge of the financial sector and strong technical knowledge with regard to machine and deep learning that can lead to practical, usable regulatory and supervisory tools with enhanced predictive ability.

Clearly, RegTech is in its infancy and requires significant effort, from both regulators and supervisors and RegTech firms, before greater strides can be made with regard to use of machine and deep learning in regulation and supervision (of financial services) and to specifically achieve the objectives set out above—i.e., provide early warning signals of key aspects going wrong and periodic information on exceptions in key factors, both with a view to preempt and prevent a financial crisis.

Let me give you some examples here.

One aspect is the need for smart tools to isolate the impact of compensation—in financial conglomerates, investment and commercial banks and other financial institutions—in terms of whether they are rewarding the quick deal and short-term gain, without consideration of the long-term consequences. In my opinion, the tool should be able to decipher from the maze of data available whether the compensation system and incentives encouraged the big bet—right from senior management through middle to lower management levels—that, in turn, would have a ripple effect on the organizational culture in terms of enhancing needless risk taking. Learning from past crisis situations, without a doubt, regulators and supervisors have to be most concerned with this and RegTech would be playing a crucial and proactive role in regulation and supervision if it can indeed help spot these trends early. The case of the 2007/8 U.S. subprime financial crisis—where compensation systems directly led to the crisis by encouraging short-term performance with unheard of incentives and compensation, when, in reality, the risks were mostly medium- and long-term—is still fresh in our memories. Therefore, smart tools from RegTech will go a long way in helping to understand compensation trends and patterns as they arise and help keep in check excessive risk taking by firms, that leads to crisis situations. In fact, the presence of such a tool will help make regulation and supervision more effective, efficient and timely in terms of action on the ground.

Yet another example comes from the FCIC report[2]: "In the years leading up to the crisis, too many financial institutions, as well as too many households, borrowed to the hilt, leaving them vulnerable to

---

[2] 'Financial Crisis Inquiry Report, Final Report of the National Commission on the Causes of the Financial and Economic Crisis in the United States', The Financial Crisis Inquiry Commission, 2011, http://fcic-static.law.stanford.edu/cdn_media/fcic-reports/fcic_final_report_full.pdf

financial distress or ruin if the value of their investments declined even modestly. For example, as of 2007, the five major investment banks—Bear Stearns, Goldman Sachs, Lehman Brothers, Merrill Lynch, and Morgan Stanley—were operating with extraordinarily thin capital. By one measure, their leverage ratios were as high as 40 to 1, meaning for every $ 40 in assets, there was only $ 1 in capital to cover losses. Less than a 3% drop in asset values could wipe out a firm. To make matters worse, much of their borrowing was short-term, in the overnight market—meaning the borrowing had to be renewed each and every day. For example, at the end of 2007, Bear Stearns had $ 11.8 billion in equity and $ 383.6 billion in liabilities and was borrowing as much as $ 70 billion in the overnight market. It was the equivalent of a small business with $ 50,000 in equity borrowing $ 1.6 million, with $ 296,750 of that due each and every day."

And what needs to be noted here is that this leverage was well disguised and hidden—in derivatives positions, in off-balance-sheet entities, through window dressing of financial reports, etc. Thus, a smart tool to help unearth the (real) hidden leverage of investment banks and other financial institutions would add great value. This again, is a great opportunity to create smart tools for better and more effective regulation and supervision.

The crucial aspect of conflicts of interest, which were responsible for the 2008 financial crisis, is another case in point. Conflicts of interests are indeed a major regulatory concern because where conflicts of interest exist corruption[3] could rear its ugly head (if the conflicts of interest are not well identified and managed appropriately).

Here are some examples of conflicts of interest from the FCIC report—a) conflicts of interest among rating agencies in evaluating collateralized debt obligation (CDO) deals; b) underwriters assisting CDO managers in selecting collateral; c) hedge fund managers selecting collateral from their funds to place in CDOs that they offered to other investors; d) a conflict faced by a large financial conglomerate in offering 'liquidity puts' that gave it huge fees in the short term but placed significant financial risk on it in the long term; and e) the settlement that the securities and exchanges commission (SEC) reached with a large investment bank, in which that firm paid $ 550 million to settle charges filed by the SEC, and acknowledged that disclosures made in marketing a subprime mortgage product contained incomplete (potentially misleading) information.

Now, this is where RegTech could provide a smart tool that could help regulators and supervisors sift through all compliance and other data and themselves construct an 'index' of conflicts of interest—for financial conglomerates and institutions—which then could serve as the basis for an effective conflicts risk governance framework. This too represents a great chance to get analytical tools for better regulation and supervision.

---

[3] And let us be clear that where corruption exists, conflicts of interest are always there and have not been managed appropriately.

To summarize, a great opportunity exists for smart RegTech tools on lots of aspects, and regulators and supervisors could benefit from such smart tools for understanding issues that caused the 2007/8 U.S. subprime financial crisis or the 2010 Indian microfinance crisis in Andhra Pradesh or the 2018 banking crisis in India (the case of fraudulent and fake letters of understanding issued by the Punjab National Bank in particular).

In short, RegTech could provide smart tools for understanding all the issues that caused past financial crisis situations, and there are huge untapped opportunities for RegTech firms with the resources, willingness and ability to create path-breaking applications. Thus, RegTech could help develop a large number of useful applications for central banks and other financial sector regulators and supervisors worldwide.

Before I sign off, I would like to quote Cassius from *Julius Caesar*: "The fault, dear Brutus, is not in our stars, But in ourselves."[4]

Just as the above quote argues, all of the financial crisis situations we have encountered—whether the U.S. subprime (2007/8) or the Indian microfinance crisis in Andhra Pradesh in 2010 or the recent Indian banking crisis (e.g., the LoU scam) in 2018—were not caused by computer models or algorithms or earthquakes or tsunamis. They were created by human action and inaction. All of these crisis

---

[4] See https://www.enotes.com/shakespeare-quotes/fault-dear-brutus-our-stars

situations had early warnings signals that the captains of the ship (i.e., the public stewards of the financial system) failed to read and act upon. Theirs was not a mere stumble but rather a huge missed step.

Part of the problem is that the massive burgeoning growth (be it in toxic mortgages or daily borrowings secured by these mortgages or in microfinance loans) left the already thin regulatory architecture stranded as they were perhaps dealing with larger volumes of increasingly complex sets of data, than before! RegTech, if structured to ask the right questions and bring out the right insights, could be hugely beneficial for regulators and supervisors who are already overwhelmed by such data, and the time is ripe now for RegTech to take the lead in facilitating better regulation and supervision of traditional and new age financial institutions worldwide. Otherwise, these financial institutions, which are at least perhaps ten times larger and ten times more riskier than those present in 2007/8, could cause newer crisis situations, which in turn will result in exclusion of people and thereby spoil our effort to achieve 100% sustained financial inclusion by 2030 as per SDG 1.3. And of course, if RegTech is to facilitate effective regulation and supervision in real time, the regulatory and supervisory framework must be made accountable and free of conflicts of interest—this indeed is the focus of chapter 15.

Chapter 15

Regulatory Accountability Vital for Sustained Financial Inclusion

When I started writing this book, my primary objective was to focus on inclusive finance and what is wrong with the present paradigm. The journey through this book should have certainly enabled you, the reader, to understand my perspective on the key antecedents to this and the consequences of the same.

That said, I have felt all along the need to bring a broader financial sector perspective, and position the 2007/8 U.S. subprime and 2010 Indian microfinance crisis in Andhra Pradesh (AP) and subsequent events thereafter within the ambit of the larger financial sector framework. I will try to do that in this final chapter, using central banks and their legal framework as a fulcrum for my analysis. I am sure you will find this perspective interesting, as it raises important and yet fundamental issues with regard to financial sector regulation and supervision and the conflicts of interests embedded therein.

In fact, I see 'conflicts of interest' as one of the major reasons for the lax regulation and supervision of the financial sector in U.S.A., India and elsewhere. And how this lax regulation and supervision has, in turn, impacted the financial sector is indeed well known.

Indeed, three pillars of regulatory architecture failed miserably: (i) supervision of financial entities; (ii) protection of consumers who were clients of these entities; and (iii) use of self-regulatory organizations that could do very little to actually protect the end-user (poor) clients.

And a lot of this happened because industry insiders lobbied hard to ensure 'financial innovation'. Steady regulation and supervision were objected to and booted out for the supposed benefit of enhancing financial innovation and financial inclusion.

Given this discussion, one is tempted to make the assertion that, lack of *accountability on the part of the regulators/supervisors and lack of transparency in their operations has indeed led to the present situation.*

Thus, given these factors, I strongly feel that the time is now absolutely ripe to make central banks and other financial services regulators more accountable.

With their wide-ranging powers and greater impact on all aspects of the economy, their accountability assumes even greater importance and should not be ignored. And this accountability will have to come in several transparent ways, which are discussed extensively here:

Institutional accountability, can come in two major ways: (i) short-term measures, such as making the board of the central bank/other regulators more accountable and the aspects associated with this; and (ii) long-term measures such as making the central bank and other financial services regulators directly accountable to nationally elected bodies (parliaments, U.S. Congress, etc) and the mechanisms that go with it. While it is easy to propose long-term measures and distract from the real issue at hand, in my opinion, certain short-term steps can and should be immediately taken and the Ministry of Finance must make the regulators more administratively accountable, as first highlighted.

Simple things, as given here, can be done to facilitate regulatory accountability in the short term. Just as charity begins at home, accountability must start with the regulatory boards, which is in fact the first and most important layer in a multi-layered accountability process. Long-term measures such as regulatory heads reporting to elected bodies (parliament or U.S. Congress) and other similar aspects can happen eventually. However, there are low hanging fruits to be plucked and they need to be harvested right away (in the short-term) with regard to the issue of making regulators more accountable.

Therefore, central banks,[1] that have been created by society at large (and not just governments or politicians), have one key objective. They must preserve the value of the currency which they have been mandated to issue for use by all of us.

I emphasize maintenance in value because any erosion of this value would mean that we, the people, would lose the overall value of our wealth. To me, that would amount to a betrayal of the trust which, we, the people, have placed in the central bank. And in my opinion, this trust cannot be built either by government ownership of the central bank or the laws that have helped establish it, but rather by the efficiency, professionalism, integrity, and adherence to good governance by those who run the central bank. And of those who run the central bank, the most important, in my opinion, is the board, which is sacrosanct and must be maintained so. Thus, the first line of accountability would have to be the board of the central bank and it must be made accountable to the people in the respective countries. That said, what then are the changes required to ensure this?

Specifically, this, in effect, would translate into the following:

a. *Using the board as the key evaluator of central bank's performance:* Treating the board as the key evaluator of the central bank's performance[2] and

---

[1] While many arguments have been made in relation to central banks, the same applies to other financial service regulators as well.
[2] Other than monetary policy, which would have to be dealt with separately!

that of the governor (both as a leader and manager). The nonexecutive (independent) members must be capable of performing this task appropriately and independently. At a later stage, the central bank could even consider the establishment and use of an independent 'lead nonexecutive director' position and facilitate regular independent meetings of the nonexecutive directors (alone) so that the above is achieved in an objective manner.

b. *Ensuring a transparent board appointment process:* Competency-based processes must be used for the selection of people (who have the capacity, ethics, skills, and orientation) to serve on the central board. Filling up vacancies on the central bank board should thus be through proper procedure, involving a search and selection committee with at least two to four names being proposed for each board vacancy. The finance ministry (or treasury department or equivalent) in the respective country can easily do this and thereby set the highest standards of corporate governance to the central bank as an institution. If the appointment of board members is compromised, then corporate governance and accountability of the central bank as an institution (and, more importantly, as the country's central bank) would suffer, as seems to have been the case in many situations. Proper attention must be paid to taking care of the reverse revolving door phenomenon.

Thus, the need of the hour is a transparent board appointment policy for the central bank and this policy must also ensure that directors have adequate skills and experience (apart from the availability of time to do their job effectively). The policy must also ensure that the overall composition of the central bank's board of directors is suitably diverse—including more women, youth, and individuals with the requisite skills (and appropriate backgrounds) on the central bank board is perhaps a way to improve the board's overall functioning and effectiveness. The policy must also ensure that conflict of interest issues are taken into account with regard to board appointments, so that the independence of the nonexecutive directors is not compromised under any circumstances (whatsoever).

c. *Establishing critical non-negotiables for board composition:* People who have an ongoing direct commercial interest in the provision of financial services (through banking companies, NBFIs, equity investments in such institutions and other related institutions) should *not* be appointed to the board of the central bank. This single step should go a long way to enhancing the accountability of the central bank as an institution and must be implemented forthwith. Likewise, relatives and/or very close friends of the central bank staff *(including the governor or deputy governors and their equivalents, executive directors and other board members)* should *not* be appointed to the central bank board. Similarly, it may be wise to keep politicians out of the central bank board. Let me make one thing clear here. This is not an exhaustive list of non-negotiables. Rather, it must be viewed as a starter set that provides examples of the kinds of relationships that are better avoided to enable effective functioning of the central bank board and, more importantly, facilitate public confidence with regard to the same.

Otherwise, serious conflicts of interests and related situations, as has happened in past crisis situations could happen here, much to the detriment of the reputation of the central bank. This is not to be construed that people with a background in economics, finance, business administration, and related areas should not be appointed to the central bank board. They can be, provided they meet the minimum non-negotiable criteria, such as those mentioned. In fact, the Financial Sector Legislative Reforms Commission in India has made (similar) good suggestions in this regard.[3]

---

[3] I have adapted Clause 2 (c) to include any financial service provider.
"9. (1) Members of the Reserve Bank Board must be fit and proper persons, having expertise in dealing with matters relating to banking, payments and monetary
(2) A person cannot be appointed as a member on the Reserve Bank Board if such
(a) is an employee of the Central Government, except in the case of the nominee members;
(b) is a member of Parliament or a state legislature;
(c) is a director, employee or officer of any banking or financial service provider;
(d) is a director, employee or officer of any system provider;
(e) is a member of an advisory council of the Reserve Bank; or
(f) is a member of the Monetary Policy Committee, other than –
    (i) the Reserve Bank Chairperson; or

Look at it this way. The central bank is the regulator and supervisor of the financial sector in the respective countries and the board is involved in many critical deliberations related to the financial sector. What assurance can the central bank board provide that these important discussions and decisions will not be shared by nonexecutive directors with their parent (or related) organizations that have some form of commercial interest in the financial sector? In fact, providing central board membership to anyone connected with institutions that have a strong commercial interest in the financial sector will, for the above-mentioned reasons, give undue advantage to these institutions as they will gain access to what economists often call *superior information*.

And this is not to say that people who have in the past served in organizations with a commercial interest in the financial sector cannot become board members of the central bank. Maintaining a requisite cooling period of between 3–5 years before they are appointed to the central bank board seems an advisable strategy. All in all, it would be prudent and appropriate if those with strong, ongoing commercial interests in the financial sector are not made board members of the central bank.

(ii) the executive member designated by the Reserve Bank Board to serve on the Monetary Policy Committee."

d. *Circumscribing the term of a central bank board member:* Restricting board terms for people (on the central bank board) to a maximum of 8 years (at the most, 2 terms of four years each) and ensuring regular induction of new members is critical. When board members get older than the furniture in the boardroom, experience suggests that they could be compromised in different ways and, therefore, 'unrestricted board terms' as practice, is better avoided. This needs to be implemented immediately at all central banks.

e. *Facilitating evaluation of board member performance:* Having a compulsory formal evaluation of the functioning of the central bank's board of directors by an external independent evaluator is necessary. And the results of this evaluation should be made available to the public—officially publishing the evaluation (on their website) is an aspect that could also be considered by the concerned central bank. It goes without saying that independent evaluators—individuals and/or institutions—must not have had a material relationship (as defined in common parlance) with the central bank.

f. *Ensuring that central bank board members do not get involved in non-board activities:* Ensuring that board members do not head or serve on other central bank committees (outside of the board) concurrently is a very important issue. The central bank board's primary task, as noted earlier, is very clear—to monitor the central bank's performance and that of its executives, including the governor, deputy governor (or equivalents), and act as the first stage of defence in the multi-layered accountability mechanism. That being the case, they cannot and should not serve on any committees other than board subcommittees as they would, as part of the board duties, have a role in evaluating the functioning of these committees.

g. *Reducing key person dependence:* Key person dependence at central banks is especially common. This is clearly bad practice of corporate governance and it reduces the accountability of the central bank as an institution. With all due respect, I am not sure that any central bank is acting with accountability, when it puts a single board member on many non-board committees and panels, *which the board (of which (s) he is part of) will ultimately have to evaluate!* And matters get worse if the person concerned has links with commercial entities involved with the financial services sector, as undue conflicts of interest will arise.

h. *Emphasizing procedural accountability:* If you look at the lessons from the global subprime crisis (and the same is true of the Andhra Pradesh 2010 microfinance crisis), a key aspect is procedural accountability whereby professionals with an active commercial interest in the financial sector are neither made part of the central bank board nor committees recommending regulation for the sector.

i. *Adopting an official formal code of conduct publicly:* Lastly, an official code of conduct needs to be *formally* and publicly adopted by the central bank board with regard to various aspects, including activities and roles that board members can engage in (as board members of the central bank) and disclosures to be made to them with regard to conflicts of interest and several other issues.

Overall, what needs to be emphasized here is that central banks have fair practice and other codes for various stakeholders including banks, NBFIs and others. Is it not fair that the central bank has an official code adopted formally for its board and staff? And once adopted formally, it should be available publicly and board members would have to make appropriate disclosures as per the code. This is a very simple task to set the ball rolling for greater institutional accountability and central bank heads must push hard to get this done quickly so that *the central bank indeed becomes the change that it wants to ultimately see on the ground in its countries financial sector.*

Thus, accountability and ethics are crucial to the survival of the financial sector and there is no doubt that there has been a systemic breakdown in accountability and ethics globally across the financial sector in the past few years, leading to various forms of economic crises, the effects of which we are still experiencing! As all of you would agree, the integrity and credibility of financial markets and peoples' trust in these markets are of paramount importance to the economic health of countries—there is no exception to this basic dictum. And therefore, without any doubt, the stability, soundness, safety and sustained prosperity of each and every country's financial system and larger economy rely fundamentally on the notions of fairness, transparency, and accountability. In other words, central banks must ensure this happens consistently at all levels in the financial sector, whereby the concerned stakeholders (be it regulators, supervisors, banks, NBFIs, new age FIs, FinTech firms, MFIs, and others) produce services of high quality and conduct themselves fairly and with a high degree of transparency and accountability.

And the central bank in each respective country must start to facilitate this process of metamorphosis, which is required *now*, more than ever before! In other words, unless the central bank and other financial service regulators become the change they want to see in the financial sector, I am afraid that there will be very little action on the ground in terms of accountability. And without accountability and ethics among financial service regulators, reaching our desired goal of 100% sustained financial inclusion by 2030 as per SDG 1.3, would become a very onerous task indeed.

Chapter 16

Conclusion

Financial inclusion is the buzzword of today. Yet, we know very little of financial inclusion. For one, neither I nor anyone can put an accurate count on the number of mutually exclusive financially included people (globally as well as by country) at this moment—this is despite trillions of dollars flowing through the financial system on a yearly basis and billions of dollars being invested in efforts to financially include excluded people.

Why is this so?

There are critical reasons for this. One, financial inclusion is yet to be defined in a consistent manner across a wide variety of financial services—this is true globally as well as across individual countries. The implications of this are that there are no reliable and valid measures of financial inclusion as of now.

Two, financial inclusion is a dynamic, highly individual, specific phenomenon. Therefore, people get financially included, excluded, re-included and this goes on in a dynamic cycle. That is why it is crucial that we get an accurate handle on the actual number of mutually exclusive financially included people at any moment, anywhere globally.

Three, financial inclusion is not *just* about low-income people or bottom of the pyramid clients anymore, despite their obvious importance. It is about every mutually exclusive individual (irrespective of ethnicity, color, religion, gender, age, class, caste, etc.) having continuous opportunities to access a wide variety of need-based, affordable, financial services delivered through traditional and new age financial institutions in a sustainable, transparent and accountable manner.

Given the above, the question is how to track progress towards the set goal of 100% (sustained) financial inclusion by 2030 as per SDG 1.3. Do we know where we are today worldwide (with regard to that goal)? My answer is an emphatic no. We have no idea (whatsoever) about the number of mutually exclusive individuals who are financially included (worldwide) at any time, let alone in a certain period.

Having said that, do we know where we want to be by 2030? Yes, we desire to have 100% (sustained) financial inclusion (worldwide) as per SDG 1.3. Do we know how to get from 'where we are' to 'where we want to be by 2030'? My answer is a strong no because if we don't know 'where we are today', we won't know how to reach 'where we want to be by 2030'.

Do we have indicators that will tell us whether we have reached the point 'where we want to be by 2030'? My answer is a big no, as we have neither a precise definition of financial inclusion nor reliable or valid measures of this dynamic construct. And tracking mutually exclusive individuals is still a huge part of problem.

Can we do something before it is too late? Of course, and to achieve the above, countries around the globe must do the following:

1. Every country must implement a unique ID scheme based on biometric identification[1] so that each and every individual has a unique identifier,
2. Every country must define financial inclusion in accordance with global standards (as articulated in chapters 3 and 4 of this book) and relevance to their country's context. This will include definition of when one is financially included, excluded and so on,
3. Every country must link delivery of every financial inclusion service with the unique ID, so that every financial transaction is linked to a unique ID. The unique ID will also serve to eliminate population census, income tax unique number, voter ID and so on. These are the huge savings expected from this,

---

[1] Alternatives to finger prints would be eye scans and voice recognition. These can also be used.

4. The unique ID will be on a permissioned blockchain established by the government/central bank/other financial service regulators. It will work on a dual key mechanism—a public key (with the government/central bank/other financial service regulators) and also a private key (with the concerned individual). The private key would be mandatorily required to access any individual's data—in that way, the privacy aspects would be taken care of. Thus, the private key will be with the concerned individual who will, de facto, control access to their own data,
5. All financial transactions pertaining to an individual will be stored on a chip-based unique ID card and it will also be on the permissioned blockchain, which, unlike a central server, is less amenable to hacking,
6. This way, we can get to know anytime, anywhere, financial inclusion in every country and globally.

By anytime, anywhere reliable and valid population level financial institution data on mutually exclusive individuals, I am talking of the following:

- Actual number of mutually exclusive individuals who are included at the beginning of any financial year or specified period,
- Actual number of mutually exclusive individuals who are included during any financial year or specified period,
- Actual number of mutually exclusive individuals—financially included at the beginning of the financial year or specified period—who

were forced to exit the financial system during the financial year or specified period,
- Actual number of mutually exclusive individuals who are included at the end of any financial year or specified period.

One point is in order here. It is very important to look at the traditional financial inclusion paradigm—which assumes many things—and analyze it objectively. We first need to question which of those assumptions work in real time.

For example, one assumption is that people, once financially included, always stay included, but this is a misleading assumption. I have come across so many people who have been included once but were excluded later. Why don't we have measures and studies that look at people who have been included once but excluded later? Conversely, why don't we have measures of people who have been excluded earlier and included later? And do we really know how many people leave the financial ecosystem because of the financial products (goods and services), processes, distribution mechanisms and delivery channels that we have designed for use? I have not come across any real large scale studies on this! Furthermore, why people get excluded after being financially included is an aspect that would provide tremendous value to the design and delivery of financial inclusion services (including digital financial inclusion).

Yet another assumption of the traditional financial inclusion paradigm is that the people included are always 'new' or 'fresh' to financial inclusion. That is the way to bolster the outreach[2] data, so necessary for showing that financial inclusion works! That financial inclusion is important is an aspect that needs no debate. It is clear and has been long settled! But it is not the be all or end all of everything! Many other things need to be in place for financial inclusion to be effective and sans these, the real impact of financial inclusion may never be felt. What we need to know clearly is how our financial inclusion efforts pan out in real time in any given financial year: a) How many people who are included stay included during the year; b) How many people who have been included during the year were previously included in earlier years and then

---

[2] Let me give you an example of what happens with outreach data, taking a country like India. Please note that some of these financial inclusion services could be one-time services (like going to an ombudsman), others (like loans) may be repeat services, and some others like savings accounts (or pension accounts) could even be continuous long-term services, which are consistently used. Likewise, several institutions may combine to form a channel—*for example, I could get a loan from a SHG that is linked to a bank which has been refinanced by a DFI like NABARD*. I could also get a loan from an MFI that has borrowed from a DFI (SIDBI) and is on-lending to me. The permutations and combinations are endless here, but please note that the above distinction between channels and institutions is very important for determining the correct outreach of financial inclusion! In fact, the real outreach of our financial inclusion services through the various channels and institutions is not transparently known today. This is because there is an overstatement of outreach figures through double and triple counting as sometimes data from different institutions within a channel is added up to give an incorrect outreach figure. Sometimes, people have genuinely accessed services through different channels as well. This again provides an exaggerated picture of total outreach and penetration with regard to financial inclusion. And only reliable and valid outreach data will help us track progress towards financial inclusion, specifically in terms of SDG 1.3.

subsequently excluded; c) How many people who have been included are fresh inclusions to the financial world; d) How many people who were previously included in the preceding year have been excluded this year and why.

And once this is all done we will be able to have reliable and valid anytime, anywhere, population level financial inclusion data on mutually exclusive individuals, which in turn will help us track progress and perform on-course correction towards SDG 1.3—which is 100% sustained financial inclusion by 2030.

Clearly, many other things are required to happen as corollaries if we are to achieve our goal of 100% sustained financial inclusion by 2030:

a) We need to ensure that all our efforts to financially include excluded people do *not* result in crisis situations that in reality undermine our *efforts* to include people financially. I am specifically talking of the U.S. subprime (2007/8) and the Indian microfinance crisis in Andhra Pradesh (2010), both of which had common themes—burgeoning growth, poor governance, weak risk management, opportunistic compensation and wrong incentives, inappropriate products and systems, and so on.

In other words, we need to ensure that there are appropriate checks and balances—both within the financial system and among those who oversee it—for any large-scale effort that we may take to financially include excluded people. Among other things, this calls for improved regulation and supervision without conflicts of interest, which indeed have to be eliminated at all levels, including in the financial system. The other key aspect is the use of RegTech for getting early warning signals as well as creating a solid regulatory/supervisory framework in the wake of burgeoning data available on large number of traditional and new age financial institutions that carry greater risk as well. Furthermore, at all of these financial institutions, it also calls for sound independent internal audits and better governance (at all levels), prudent risk management and appropriate systems for compensation. Several chapters in this book highlight the key issues related to the above—see chapters 9, 10, 11 and 12.

b) We also need to ensure that innovative approaches/platforms, including FinTech and blockchains (DLT), are strongly nurtured and encouraged. While they indeed carry some risks, the new age institutions that utilize them, as noted above, must be subject to good governance, prudent risk management, transparent and fair compensation and independent internal audits, as articulated in chapters 9, 10, 11 and 12. That is a non-negotiable if we are to move towards 100% sustained financial inclusion by 2030.

That is not all. With disruptive and transformative technology like blockchains and artificial intelligence likely to have a greater influence on corporate strategy going forward, it will become important from a strategic perspective for traditional and new age financial institutions to have a Chief Environmental Scanning Officer reporting directly to the board on trends (that could impact their businesses): a) technology; b) climate change; c) political risk; and d) regulatory risk, etc.

As Miles & Snow (1978) had conceptualized, following on the great footsteps of Alfred Chandler & Herbert Simon, organizations can no longer "defend" domains (read markets), assuming that the "world of tomorrow" will be the "same as today." Rather, they have to be prospectors that thrive and create the uncertainty and disruption that is prevalent (in markets) today. Or they have to be differentiated defenders (a hybrid based on the Miles & Snow (1978) typology combined with that of Mike Porter[3]) that guard their relatively stable domains in a differentiated manner while remaining extremely vigilant to changing environments. Strategic choices in many industries—information technology, banking, finance etc—are going to be dictated by disruptive/transformative innovation and organizations must be prepared to tackle this head-on in a proactive manner.

c) That is not all. Vulnerability reducing and bargaining/negotiating power enhancing financial

---

[3] See appendix 2.

products and services must also be available at an affordable cost and appropriate scale for all people.

People have been asking me for an example of vulnerability reducing financial services. Here is one we piloted. The key is to look for points in supply chains where vulnerability can be mitigated and the bargaining, negotiating and staying power of small producers and informal sector micro, small and medium enterprises (MSME's) can be enhanced.

Take a vegetable vendor who typically sells from street platforms. When is she vulnerable? At the end of the day!!! She will sell you everything she has left for small change. What we did was something simple. Simple cold storages were created and leased to vendors for a monthly rent. All of a sudden, women who were selling their entire leftovers for small change started feeling empowered and refused to do so, as they could store their leftovers and come and sell these the next day. A simple intervention changed many lives.

Imagine if this can be scaled up worldwide for all kinds of vendors (especially with perishables)—those who sell on platforms, through pushcarts, etc.,—that indeed would have a great impact. There is so much that can be done in many supply chains. Little things that can make a huge difference, and the financial inclusion industry is the right one that can usher in these changes.

Likewise, untapped MSME's are a huge market. I have been seeing a lot of excluded MSME's in what we call the informal sector. I did see a lot of similar MSME's when I conducted a study for the National Commission on Enterprises in the Unorganized Sector in 2008 and also subsequently when I worked for the Commonwealth Secretariat in Uganda (2011), St Lucia (2009) and Malawi (2008). I also saw a lot of these MSMEs when I did a study of them in seven countries during the period 2014-2016. And of course, I have been seeing a lot of these MSMEs in India, post demonetization (November 2016).

These MSME's typically borrow in the range of U.S. $ 1,000 to U.S. $ 50,000 (they are often called the missing middle). They have an excellent repayment record (as borne by their bank statements or equivalent) and they usually repay in loan terms of 5-6 months (primarily through checks [cheques] and similar banking instruments). These MSMEs, which can be found in the metros and small shanty towns, are served primarily by the local informal sector moneylenders who know them well and visit them often with their agents.

And unfortunately, despite the so-called growth of universal financial services, many of these enterprises borrow at rates greater than 95% APR (annualized percentage rate)—a lot of the times the interest is taken upfront. In my opinion, these MSME's are a fantastic market for traditional and new age financial institutions—be it small finance banks, NBFIs and FinTech firms—who are interested in asset-based financing. I am somewhat surprised that the formal financial sector is yet to touch many such MSME's in many countries.

Thus, regardless of increasing credit to MSMEs and agriculture over the years, we are yet to see its real impact on the ground. Part of the reason is that we assume that more credit to agriculture and MSMEs is better, but experience shows that 'quality credit' is what makes a difference.

By quality credit, I am talking of vulnerability reducing financial services (not the usual ineffective agriculture insurance or similar products for MSMEs) that enhance the staying, bargaining and negotiating power of small producers across the supply chain, including post-harvest and post production financing—another example would be well-designed and safely implemented warehouse receipt financing at scale. Neither the government nor the private sector can do this by themselves. We need public-private community partnerships (PPCPs) to achieve this on a country wide scale across sub-sectors globally and this again would go a long way in ensuring 100% sustained financial inclusion by 2030.

Lastly, some specific comments are in order before I sign off for one final time.

Powering A Billion Dreams

We must start to produce results in terms of strengthening livelihoods as well as creating new jobs. Poverty and inequity can be found in large, large numbers. Indebtedness on the average is rising and rising fast, *ceteris paribus*. Central banks, other financial service regulators, DFIs, various kinds of FIs, including commercial banks and new age FinTech companies, bilaterals, multilaterals and others traditional financial institutions, governments and stakeholders have the resources to wipe out poverty and root out inequity—yet, their projects don't do that. This is because the gap between intended and realized strategies is huge. It is about time for all these stakeholders to take the bull by the horns. Poverty can be rooted out and inequity eliminated. We need new, innovative and bold approaches not bound by bureaucratic shackles—time to act now and act decisively.

Billions of dollars have flowed to get people out of poverty. And while extreme poverty is reported to have been halved over 25 years from the early 1990s, real progress on the ground is questionable. People remain hugely vulnerable to falling back into poverty. Not just that, rising inequality threatens democracies worldwide. The time has come now to act and act resolutely, and we need a serious paradigm shift in our approach to poverty alleviation and inequality, if UN SDGs (1 and 10) are to be met. This paradigm shift must view poverty as a cycle and a dynamic construct. This will help us devise strategies that can create wealth at the grass roots through unconventional approaches that can result in sustainable livelihoods and permanent jobs for millions and millions of people.

Such approaches must also focus on mechanisms that can prevent people lifted out of extreme poverty from becoming poor again. As noted above, the key to poverty alleviation and tackling inequality is wealth creation at grass roots, just as in the game of cricket, the key to stopping a 'flow of runs' is the taking of wickets. We need daring, avant-garde and practical approaches to wealth creation at the grass roots at a very large scale. We have tried everything so far and there's no harm in giving this our best shot now. It is now or never.

When people talk of extreme poverty having been halved in the last 25 years, I'd like to remind them that many of the people who supposedly have moved out of extreme poverty, are still very vulnerable to falling back into poverty again. Imperfect markets are the primary cause of this. Without a doubt, coupled with extraneous, climate change and disaster-related events, imperfect markets can easily push many of the people back into extreme poverty again. Added to this is the fact of ever-growing global inequality.

Indeed all of the above require a solid paradigm shift in financial inclusion, which should hopefully be able to enhance the bargaining, staying and negotiating power of all the people vulnerable to slipping back into poverty. And as I have said time and again, new technology like blockchains and FinTech, if structured appropriately and managed well for their (inherent) risks, can play a huge enabling role in all of this. I hope that the powers that be attend to this aspect immediately and set financial inclusion on the right track, so that it can enable millions and millions of people to combat poverty and growing inequality in an effective and permanent manner.

Two more comments are in order here. One, while poverty and extreme versions of it continue to plague the world and have to be tackled on a war footing, an equally pressing problem is the fact that growing 'inequity' gets amplified by the transparent flow of information today. When more people (be it small or large farmers, fisherfolk, MSMEs and even service providers) see that they are not getting commensurate value to what they produce, there is social tension and discontent.

And the best way to handle this is to transform supply chains from their inefficient form of operations (today) to something that is fundamentally different, more mutually beneficial and value enhancing for all stakeholders concerned. Strategies that can transform supply chains and help achieve this are: a) provision of appropriate (vulnerability reducing) finance to enhance the staying and negotiating power of vulnerable stakeholders; b) use of decentralized and value-enhancing technologies like blockchains that will enhance the transparency and accountability of supply chains. If this happens, the global movement towards achieving SDGs will be faster and on a more secure footing. Governments, central banks, multi-laterals, private sector and others must thus start to push the use of vulnerability reducing financial services and blockchains as part of supply chain development globally.

Two, for this to happen in real time, design thinking[4] has to be employed. The core of design thinking lies in the ability to create and invent a future based on an understanding of customer experiences, using (not just) empathy but also insight. In essence, design thinking calls for studying and understanding customers (with empathy and insight/knowledge) in their natural contexts.

In fact, traditional and new age financial institutions that seek deep knowledge about their customers may be better off in not just relying on big data and the standard analytics and market research tools that go with them, as they simply cannot reveal deep insights with regard to a customer's true motivations for purchasing/using a product/service and the associated challenges/constraints therein, etc.

It is only design thinking which uses empathy plus insight that can illuminate customer experiences in all their grandeur and richness. Without a doubt, the resulting knowledge can truly transform corporate strategy, organizational culture, and even the product

---

[4] In my opinion, the best example of application of design thinking in the field of low income finance was by Brij Mohan Gupta, former executive director of Small Industries Development Bank of India (SIDBI), when he was at the helm. He pioneered several innovative products including the transformation loan—which was a quasi-equity product—that enabled the many not-for-profit MFIs to seamlessly transform to NBFIs. This single step played a very important role in the scaling up of the Indian microfinance sector.

market strategy of those institutions engaged in delivering a range of inclusive finance services. And, most importantly, the dynamic nature of financial inclusion where people get excluded and included in cyclical fashion, customer protection issues and the like are best addressed through the use of design thinking tools.

And only all of the above can help us reach our dream of 100% sustained financial inclusion by 2030 in accordance with SDG 1.3. To summarize, it's now or never to end this cycle of inclusion, exclusion, re-inclusion and have sustained financial inclusion for all people, irrespective of ethnicity, gender, religion, age, economic status, class, caste and the like. Better late than never!

Appendix 1

Published Books, Articles, Papers & Unpublished Reports

Published Books (Not-Exhaustive)

1. Arunachalam Ramesh S (2017), "The Cinderella Notes: Demonetization and the Indian Economy", *SMW*, Chennai and *Createspace*, USA. See *reviews* on amazon.in and by Matthew S Gamser at amazon.com. See Prof Malcolm Harper's Review and See Sukhwinder Arora's Review of this book. This is a critically acclaimed and hugely popular book and had 2 chapters devoted to regulation and supervision of commercial banks, NBFCs, Cooperatives etc—in relation to inclusive finance (MSME, agri, micro and other pro-poor/rural financial services)
2. Arunachalam Ramesh S (2015), "Where Angels Prey", *Authors Upfront, Delhi*. See review of this book by Tim Kelley, who called it a modern day version of Pearl S Buck's "Good Earth"— https://forextv.com/top-news/book-review-where-angels-prey-by-ramesh-s-arunachalam/
3. Arunachalam, Ramesh S (2014), "An Idea Which Went Wrong: Commercial Microfinance in India", *SMW*, Chennai and *Createspace*, USA. See review of this book by Milford Bateman at http://microfinance-in-india.blogspot.in/2014/08/milford-batemans-review-of-idea-which.html
4. This again is a critically acclaimed book and held out very important lessons for banking regulation and

supervision, financial stability, safety and soundness with regard to commercial bank lending to MSME's, low income people, agriculture and the use of technology based banking. It had 12 chapters dealing with issues related to financial stability, banking regulation and supervision and the like. This books looks at ways in which the governance and accountability as also regulatory and supervisory capacities of central banks can be enhanced.

5. Arunachalam Ramesh S (2011), "The Journey of Indian Micro-Finance: Lessons For the Future" by Aapti Publications, Chennai. See amazon.in and see the review of book by Sucheta Dalal, well known journalist and managing editor *Moneylife*. This is a critically acclaimed and popular book and it offered very crucial lessons for banking regulation and supervision, financial stability, safety and soundness with regard to commercial bank lending to MSME's, low income people, agriculture and the use of technology based banking. It had 8 chapters dealing with issues related to financial stability, banking regulation and supervision and the like. This book was released by Yezdi Malegam, four time board member of the Reserve Bank of India and the author many of regulatory and supervisory laws and frameworks in India. Malegam is now heading an EXPERT COMMITTEE to look at the banking frauds, NPA situation and banking crisis in India. *See review by Milford Bateman*

Published/Other Papers (Non-Exhaustive):
1. Arunachalam Ramesh S (2008) "Micro-finance and Innovative Financing for Gender Equality: Approaches, Challenges and Strategies" for 8 WAMM Commonwealth Ministers Meeting", Uganda

2. Arunachalam Ramesh S (2008), "Scoping Paper on Financial Inclusion: Considerations and Recommendations for UNDP", by UNDP India
3. Arunachalam Ramesh S et al (2008) "Enhancing Financial Services Flow to Small Scale Marine Fisheries Sector in India", A Study for FAO/UNTRS
4. Arunachalam Ramesh S (2008) "Micro-Pensions in India: Critical Issues, Challenges and Strategies for Future" Study for MicroNed Network, Netherlands
5. Arunachalam Ramesh S (2009) "Financial Inclusion of Agriculture: Key Challenges and Ways Ahead for Agricultural Finance", Chapter in a Book on Financial and Social Inclusion Edited by Ms Smita Premchander et al, DFID WORLP Project, Orissa
6. Arunachalam Ramesh S et al (2009), "Marketing, Technology and Finance Constraints Related to MSMEs in India: A Status Report of 32 Sectors", Prepared for the National Commission on Enterprises in the Unorganised Sector (NCEUS), Government of India, New Delhi
7. Arunachalam Ramesh S (2009) "Distribution of Micro-Insurance: Key Challenges and Regulatory Recommendations", Paper published in the Issue of Journal of Insurance, Pravarthak, February 2009.
8. Arunachalam Ramesh S (2008) "UNDP Financial Inclusion Strategy in 7 Focus States: Strategic Consideration and Suggestions", UNDP
9. Arunachalam Ramesh S (2008) "Delivering Vulnerability Reducing Financial Services in an Inclusive Manner: Lessons from Commonwealth Countries for Building A Sustainable and Responsive Microfinance Portfolio", Commonwealth Secretariat and Govt. of Singapore (Paper Presented at Singapore)
10. Arunachalam Ramesh S (2008) "Microfinance and Technology—Critical Issues, Lessons and Future Implications", Paper first written for the

Microfinance India *Conference*, Oct 9 – 10th, 2007 New Delhi and subsequently revised significantly and published as part of the CORDAID Research Series, Netherlands

11. Arunachalam Ramesh S et al (2008), "Microfinance and Economic Security: Towards a New Financial Inclusion Paradigm", Paper presented at the *South Asia International Economic Security Conference*, Feb 17–20th, 2008 New Delhi
12. Arunachalam Ramesh S et al (2008), "Urban Poverty, MSMEs, Livelihoods and Microfinance: Critical Issues, Challenges and Strategies for Future", Paper presented at the Urban Poverty *International Conference*, Jan 21st–22nd, 2008, Ahmedabad, India
13. Arunachalam Ramesh S (2008), "Using Technology to Enable Formal Financial Institutions to Deliver Pro-Poor Market Based Financial Services: Areas for Regulatory Reform with Lessons from 4 years of FDCF (DFID) Implementation in India" for Ministry of Finance (MoF), Reserve Bank of India (RBI) and Insurance Regulatory Development Authority (IRDA)
14. Arunachalam, Ramesh S (2009), "The Impact of Financial Crisis on MSMEs and Micro-finance: Strategic Lessons from India, Philippines, Indonesia, Afghanistan, Kenya, Malawi and St Lucia, MCG Paper
15. Arunachalam Ramesh S (2008) "Consolidated Baseline Data on MSME and Financial Service Providers and Institutions in 7 UNDAF States", UNDP
16. Arunachalam Ramesh S (2007) et al, "India Country Scan for Financial Services Design/Delivery to Low Income People", MicroNed Netherlands
17. Brij Mohan, Ramesh S Arunachalam, Vinod Jain and NN Sharma, (2006b), "Micro-Enterprise Challenge

Fund (MECF) Design Study for CORDAID", CORDAID, Netherlands
18. Y S P Thorat and Ramesh S Arunachalam-(2005), "Regulation And Areas Of Potential Market Failure In Micro-Finance", Paper Presented at NABARD High Level Policy Conference, New Delhi
19. Arunachalam Ramesh S (2005) "A Comprehensive MIS Toolkit for Financial Services Delivery for Low Income People: A Step by Step Guide for Implementation", MCG, India
20. Arunachalam Ramesh S (2001) "Designing and Implementing an MIS for Micro-finance: Key Strategies and Guidelines", Paper presented at SIDBI–BIRD Annual Conference and published as a chapter in book by published by BIRD (Bankers Institute of Rural Development)

Published Articles Related To Regulation/ Supervision, Governance, Digitization and Financial Stability

1. Arunachalam, Ramesh (2013), 'Should the RBI be made more accountable?—Part1', October 17, 2013, *Moneylife,* https://www.moneylife.in/article/should-the-rbi-be-made-more-accountable-mdashpart1/34926.html
2. Arunachalam, Ramesh (2013), 'How the RBI can be made more accountable – Part 2', October 24, 2013, *Moneylife,* https://www.moneylife.in/article/how-the-rbi-can-be-made-more-accountable-ndash-part-2/34996.html
3. Arunachalam, Ramesh (2013), 'How the RBI can be made more accountable— Part 3', October 31, 2013, *Moneylife,* https://www.moneylife.in/article/how-the-rbi-can-be-made-more-accountablemdash-part-3/35110.html
4. Arunachalam, Ramesh S (2012), 'Effective control systems at MIVs: The key to accountable investing

and responsible microfinance globally', 10/09/2012, *Moneylife*, http://www.moneylife.in/article/effective-control-systems-at-mivs-the-key-to-accountable-investing-and-responsible-microfinance-globally/28376.html

5. Arunachalam, Ramesh S (2012), 'Regulation and supervision of microfinance investment vehicles: A suggested practical framework—Part I', 05/09/2012, *Moneylife*, http://www.moneylife.in/article/regulation-and-supervision-of-microfinance-investment-vehicles-a-suggested-practical-frameworkmdashpart-i/28284.html

6. Arunachalam, Ramesh S (2012), 'Regulation and supervision of microfinance investment vehicles: A suggested practical framework—Part II', 06/09/2012, *Moneylife*, http://www.moneylife.in/article/regulation-and-supervision-of-microfinance-investment-vehicles-a-suggested-practical-frameworkmdash-part-ii/28314.html

7. Arunachalam, Ramesh S (2012), 'Why not regulate and supervise microfinance investment vehicles in their country of incorporation?', 20/08/2012, *Moneylife*, http://www.moneylife.in/article/why-not-regulate-and-supervise-microfinance-investment-vehicles-in-their-country-of-incorporation/27871.html

8. Arunachalam, Ramesh S (2012), 'Regulation and supervision of MIVs: An urgent task for central banks and regulators globally', 28/07/2012, *Moneylife*, http://www.moneylife.in/article/regulation-and-supervision-of-mivs-an-urgent-task-for-ral-banks-and-regulators-globally/27327.html

9. Arunachalam, Ramesh S (2012), 'Independent internal audit is the key to implementing responsible microfinance in MFIs', 12/07/2012, *Moneylife*, http://www.moneylife.in/article/independent-

internal-audit-is-the-key-to-implementing-responsible-microfinance-in-mfis/26953.html

10. Arunachalam, Ramesh S (2012), 'How to make the boards of large NBFC MFIs implement corporate governance norms in practice? (Part I)', 04/07/2012, *Moneylife*, http://www.moneylife.in/article/how-to-make-the-boards-of-large-nbfc-mfis-implement-corporate-governance-norms-in-practice-part-i/26776.html

11. Arunachalam, Ramesh S (2012), 'Corporate governance: What boards of large NBFC MFIs can do on the ground? (Part II)', 09/07/2012, *Moneylife*, http://www.moneylife.in/article/corporate-governance-what-boards-of-large-nbfc-mfis-can-do-on-the-ground-part-ii/26865.html

12. Arunachalam, Ramesh S (2012), 'Critical risk and issues in regulating bank business correspondents', 16/06/2012, *Moneylife*, http://www.moneylife.in/article/critical-risk-and-issues-in-regulating-bank-business-correspondents/26335.html

13. Arunachalam, Ramesh S (2011), 'Priority sector lending to MFIs—need for adequate supervision, December 08, 2011, *Moneylife*, http://www.moneylife.in/article/priority-sector-lending-to-mfismdashneed-for-adequate-supervision/22060.html

14. Arunachalam, Ramesh S (2011), 'The special category of NBFC MFIs: Lessons for the Department of Non-Bank Supervision, RBI' December 03, 2011, *Moneylife*, http://www.moneylife.in/article/the-special-category-of-nbfc-mfis-lessons-for-the-department-of-non-bank-supervision-rbi/21973.html

15. Arunachalam, Ramesh S (2011), 'Who Should Regulate Indian Microfinance?', November 16, 2011, *Moneylife*, http://www.moneylife.in/article/who-should-regulate-indian-micro-finance/21500.html

16. Arunachalam, Ramesh S (2011), 'MFI corporate governance norms: How can these be put in place?', September 30, 2011, *Moneylife*, http://www.moneylife.in/article/mfi-corporate-governance-norms-how-can-these-be-put-in-place/20223.html
17. Arunachalam, Ramesh S (2011), 'Establishing standards for effective management information systems for MFIs', September 12, 2011, *Moneylife*, http://www.moneylife.in/article/establishing-standards-for-effective-management-information-systems-for-mfis/19655.html
18. Arunachalam, Ramesh S (2011), 'Microfinance institutions should be permitted to transform into banks as it will help them improve services and reduce costs', August 31, 2011, *Moneylife*, http://www.moneylife.in/article/microfinance-institutions-should-be-permitted-to-transform-into-banks-as-it-will-help-them-improve-services-and-reduce-costs/19381.html
19. Arunachalam, Ramesh S (2011), 'Can the marriage of MFIs with banks be a sustainable option out of the microfinance crisis?', August 24, 2011, *Moneylife*, http://www.moneylife.in/article/can-the-marriage-of-mfis-with-banks-be-a-sustainable-option-out-of-the-microfinance-crisis/19176.html
20. Arunachalam, Ramesh S (2011), 'Never waste a crisis: Some suggested incentives for the proposed microfinance bill', August 19, 2011, *Moneylife*, http://www.moneylife.in/article/never-waste-a-crisis-some-suggested-inives-for-the-proposed-microfinance-bill/19073.html
21. Arunachalam, Ramesh S (2011), 'Four ways to improve the regulation of compensation at MFIs', August 02, 2011, *Moneylife*, http://www.moneylife.in/article/four-ways-to-

improve-the-regulation-of-compensation-at-mfis/18585.html

22. Arunachalam, Ramesh S (2011), 'Who is an independent director? Who should be treated as an independent director in NBFC MFIs?', July 29, 2011, *Moneylife*, http://www.moneylife.in/article/who-is-an-independent-director-who-should-be-treated-as-an-independent-director-in-nbfc-mfis/18517.html

23. Arunachalam, Ramesh S (2011), 'Establish standards for MFI independent directors as first step to ensure good corporate governance', July 23, 2011, *Moneylife*, http://www.moneylife.in/article/establish-standards-for-mfi-independent-directors-as-first-step-to-ensure-good-corporate-governance/18328.html

24. Arunachalam, Ramesh S (2011), 'Increasing frauds, internal lapses at MFIs: Need to strengthen supervisory arrangements to protect the poor', July 22, 2011, *Moneylife*, http://www.moneylife.in/article/increasing-frauds-internal-lapses-at-mfis-need-to-strengthen-supervisory-arrangements-to-protect-the-poor/18309.html

25. Arunachalam, Ramesh S (2011), 'Does a five-star board guarantee good corporate governance?', July 20, 2011, *Moneylife*, http://www.moneylife.in/article/does-a-five-star-board-guarantee-good-corporate-governance/18239.html

Published In *Moneylife* Magazine (Web Version). He has over 50 plus articles at *Moneylife* and other places. Several of these pertain to improving governance and accountability as also regulatory and supervisory capacities of central banks.

Appendix 2

Select Bibliography

1. Arunachalam, Ramesh S, "Madam President: History in the Making?", July 2016, Published by AuthorsUpFront
2. Arunachalam, Ramesh S, "An Idea Which Went Wrong: Commercial Microfinance in India", Published by CreateSpace, 2014
3. Arunachalam, Ramesh S, "The Journey of Indian Micro-Finance: Lessons for the Future", Published by Aapti Publications, 2011.
4. Arunachalam, Ramesh S, "Financial Inclusion of Agriculture: Key Challenges and Ways Ahead for Agricultural Finance", Edited by Ms Smita Premchander, DFID WORLP Project, 2009.
5. Arunachalam, Ramesh S, and Vipin Sharma, "Marketing, Technology and Finance Constraints Related to MSMEs in India: A Status Report of 32 Sectors", Prepared for the National Commission on Enterprises in the Unorganized Sector (NCEUS), Government of India, 2009.
6. Arunachalam, Ramesh S, "Microfinance and Innovative Financing for Gender Equality: Approaches, Challenges and Strategies", 8th Women's Affairs Ministers Meeting (WAMM), Uganda, Published by Commonwealth Secretariat, 2008.
7. Arunachalam, Ramesh S, Kurian Katticaren, V Swarup and Kalpana Iyer, "Enhancing Financial Services Flow to Small Scale Marine Fisheries

Sector—A Study for FAO/UNTRS", Published by FAO/UNTRS, 2008.
8. Arunachalam, Ramesh S, "Delivering Vulnerability Reducing Financial Services in an Inclusive Manner: Lessons from Commonwealth Countries for Building A Sustainable and Responsive Microfinance Portfolio", Commonwealth Secretariat and Govt. of Singapore (Paper Presented at Singapore) 2008.
9. Arunachalam, Ramesh S, "Microfinance and Innovative Financing for Gender Equality: Approaches, Challenges and Strategies, for 8 WAMM Commonwealth Ministers Meeting", Uganda, 2008.
10. Arunachalam Ramesh S, et al, "Microfinance and Economic Security: Towards a New Financial Inclusion Paradigm", Paper presented at the South Asia International Economic Security Conference, February 17 – 20th, 2008 New Delhi, 2008.
11. Arunachalam, Ramesh S, "Scoping Paper on Financial Inclusion: Considerations and Recommendations for UNDP", Published by UNDP, January 2008.
12. Arunachalam, Ramesh S, "UNDP Financial Inclusion Strategy in 7 Focus States: Strategic Consideration and Suggestions", UNDP, 2008.
13. Arunachalam Ramesh S et al, "Urban Poverty, MSMEs, Livelihoods and Microfinance: Critical Issues, Challenges and Strategies for Future", Paper presented at the Urban Poverty International Conference, January 21st – 22nd, 2008.

14. Arunachalam, Ramesh S, "Revisiting the Financial Inclusion Paradigm: A Review and Operationalization", MCG Working Paper, Chennai, 2007.
15. Arunachalam, Ramesh S, "Bamako 2000: Innovations in Microfinance", Technical Note 5
16. Bernard, Tara Siegel, Tiffany Hsu, Nicole Perlroth and Ron Lieber, "Equifax Says Cyberattack May Have Affected 143 Million in the U.S.", Published by The New York Times, September 2017, https://www.nytimes.com/2017/09/07/business/equifax-cyberattack.html
17. Bhandari, Bupesh, Prashanth Reddy Chintala, Vandana Gombar, Latha Jishnu, Shyamal Majumdar and Aanand Pandey "The Satyam Saga", Published by Business Standard Publication, 2009.
18. Bank for International Settlements (BIS), "Compensation and Corporate Governance", 2010
19. Burgess, Matt, "That Yahoo data breach actually hit three billion accounts", Published by *Wired*, October 2017, https://www.wired.co.uk/article/hacks-data-breaches-2017
20. Financial Crisis Inquiry Commission, "Financial Crisis Inquiry Report, Final Report Of The National Commission On The Causes Of The Financial And Economic Crisis In The United States", Submitted by The Financial Crisis Inquiry Commission, January 2011
21. *Firstpost*, "PNB case: Lapses at many levels of the bank led to country's over Rs 14,000 cr fraud,

internal report shows", June 20, 2018, https://www.firstpost.com/business/pnb-case-lapses-at-many-levels-of-the-bank-led-to-countrys-over-rs-14000-cr-fraud-internal-report-shows-4547641.html

22. Government of India, "Unique Identification Authority of India", https://www.uidai.gov.in/
23. Miles, Raymond E., Charles C. Snow, Alan D. Meyer and Henry J. Coleman, Jr, "Organizational Strategy, Structure, and Process", Published by Academy of Management, July 1978, https://www.jstor.org/stable/257544?seq=2#metadata_info_tab_contents
24. Nayak, Gayatri, "Microfinance in India is like subprime lending: Y V Reddy", November 23, 2010, *The Economic Times,* https://economictimes.indiatimes.com/news/economy/indicators/microfinance-in-india-is-like-subprime-lending-y-v-reddy/articleshow/6972903.cms
25. Reddy, Y Venugopal, "Microfinance Industry in India: Some Thoughts", October 8, 2011, *Economic & Political Weekly,* http://www.indiaenvironmentportal.org.in/files/file/microfinance.pdf
26. Reserve Bank of India (RBI), "Master Circular - Lending To Priority Sector", July 2010, https://www.rbi.org.in/Scripts/BS_ViewMasCirculardetails.aspx?id=5818
27. Reserve Bank of India (RBI), "Reserve Bank of India Act, 1934", https://rbidocs.rbi.org.in/rdocs/Publications/PDFs/RBIA1934170510.pdf

28. Reilly, Katie "Read Barack Obama's Final Speech to the United Nations as President", Published by TIME Magazine, September 20, 2016, http://time.com/4501910/president-obama-united-nations-speech-transcript/
29. Roy, Abhirup, and Aditya Kalra, "India's largest law firm facing probe in PNB fraud case", September 19, 2018, *Livemint*, https://www.livemint.com/Companies/TA0S39AzOOYENyKdesLVjP/CBI-probes-Cyril-Amarchand-in-PNB-fraud-investigation.html
30. Samuel Raja D, John, and M. Rajshekhar, "Share Microfin MD takes home Rs. 7.4 crore, more than double HDFC Bank MD's salary", The Economic Times, February 1, 2011, https://economictimes.indiatimes.com/jobs/share-microfin-md-takes-home-7-4-cr-more-than-double-hdfc-bank-mds-salary/articleshow/7401434.cms
31. Securities Exchange Commission, "The United States District Court Southern District of New York, Securities and Exchange Commission, Plaintiff, Vs. Goldman, Sachs and Co. and Fabrice Tourre, Defendants"
32. Sridhar, G. Naga, "IRDA finds "massive problems' in SKS Micro's insurance operations", May 2012, https://www.thehindubusinessline.com/money-and-banking/irda-finds-massive-problems-in-sks-micros-insurance-operations/article20436904.ece
33. The Institute of Internal Auditors, "About Internal Auditing", https://global.theiia.org/about/about-internal-auditing/Pages/About-Internal-Auditing.aspx

34. United Nations (UN), "Goal 1: End poverty in all its forms everywhere", https://www.un.org/sustainabledevelopment/poverty/
35. Wikipedia, "Aadhaar", https://en.wikipedia.org/wiki/Aadhaar

Appendix 3

The Revolving Door Phenomenon Prior to the 2007/8 U.S. Subprime Crisis

One of the biggest reasons for weak regulatory systems, prior to the 2008 financial crisis, is the near seamless shift of key people from Wall Street and private sector to regulatory and supervisory bodies through the "reverse revolving door" phenomenon.

Top executives of Wall Street firms (and representatives of special interest groups including lobbyists) have been known to take up positions in the Government or the regulatory set up.

Paulson, for example, the Treasury Secretary of the United States during the years 2006–2009 is a classic case. He came to the Treasury after nearly thirty-two years at Goldman Sachs.

Robert Rubin is yet another of those who made the switch from Wall Street to government. It must be recalled here that much of the foundation for the de-regulation that took place during former President Bill Clinton's second term, was laid during Rubin's tenure. It is, of course, common knowledge what this de-regulation ultimately did in terms of repealing the

Glass-Steagall Act, thereby resulting in the 2008 financial crisis.[1]

Often called "the reverse revolving door" phenomenon, these people have established a very strong pro-financial sector/Wall Street bias in policy formulation and regulatory enforcement by regulators and supervisors that oversee their (former) industry, former employers and/or related institutions. This oftentimes resulted in de-regulation to the detriment of the end user.

Second, is the shift of key people from government institutions to Wall Street and private sector through the normal revolving door phenomenon. There are the cases where key people from regulatory and supervisory bodies and governments have moved (either through a permanent or temporary relationship) to lucrative private-sector positions at Wall Street firms. Two examples are relevant here:

1. Paid speeches delivered by former Government position holders—all the Wall Street speeches by Hillary and Bill Clinton would come under this category; and

2. People like Lawrence Summers, Timothy Geithner, or Robert Rubin for that matter, who, after having served as Treasury Secretary, went on

---

[1] This is an opinion expressed in the final report of the Financial Crisis Enquiry Commission (FCIC), http://fcic-static.law.stanford.edu/cdn_media/fcic-reports/fcic_final_report_full.pdf

to work with Wall Street firms like D. E. Shaw, Warburg Pincus,[2] and Citigroup respectively.

Third, there have also been situations where former decision makers (including policy makers and executive decision makers) have become paid advocates and use their knowledge of and connections with governmental agencies, regulators, and supervisors to advance the interests of Wall Street companies. This again would be part of Wall Street lobbying. All of these have created significant conflicts of interests prior to the 2008 financial crisis and have been an important reason for the financial crisis having occurred itself.

---

[2] A Wall Street private equity firm

Appendix 4A

Understanding What Value Chain Finance Could Do: Key Questions to Ask?

Input Systems:
1. In general, what can be said about the input supply system in the entire chain?
2. Do the small, marginal and other primary producers and/or other chain actors have adequate access to quality inputs at reasonable prices?
3. *If not, what are the gaps in input systems and how can value chain finance help in redressing any these? If so, how and what must it specifically do to redress the constraints? Can the intervention be practically scaled up after the pilot?*

Data and Information Systems:
1. What can be said with regard to timely availability of reliable and valid production data and market/other information throughout the entire chain, for the various stakeholders?
2. *What are the gaps in information across the chain that needs to be addressed? Can value chain finance help in improving availability and flow of quality (reliable and valid) information? If so, what must it specifically do to facilitate this? Can the intervention be practically scaled up after the pilot?*

Production Systems:
1. How is primary production organized in the chain?
2. What can be said about the producers? What about their characteristics in terms of being marginal, small, medium and large producers and which of them dominates the chain in terms of various criteria—absolute number, production quality, relative power etc?
3. How and where is produce aggregated?
4. What about access to finance and BDS for primary producers and others in the chain?
5. What can be said about product quality, good practices and access to innovative technology, standards and certification in production for primary producers and others? How is new and innovative technology transferred from lab to land?
6. What is the level of (horizontal) cooperation, coordination and competition between primary producers and with other actors in the chain?
7. What is their relative (individual and collective) power of primary producers, in comparison to other stakeholders in the chain?
8. How efficient and fair are the price and terms setting mechanisms across the chain and especially from a perspective of the primary producers?
9. What about access to various markets (local, national, regional, and global) and market opportunities for the primary producers and others?

10. What about access to governmental procurement for various stakeholders including primary producers?
11. *What are the gaps in production systems in the chain and can value chain finance help in redressing any these? If so, how and what must it specifically do to redress the constraints? Can the intervention be practically scaled up after the pilot?*

Post Production Systems:
1. What systems and arrangements exist for bulking and post-harvest handling?
2. What is the level of (vertical) coordination, cooperation and competition across stakeholders in the value chain? How efficient and fair are these, especially for the primary producers?
3. Who controls the post production infrastructure and what are the consequences for the primary producers and other stakeholders in the chain?
4. What can be said about product quality, good practices and access to innovative technology, standards and certification in post production activities in the chain?
5. How is new and innovative technology transferred from lab to factory?
6. What about access to finance and BDS for post production activities in the chain?
7. What about access to various markets (local, national, regional, and global) and market opportunities for the various stakeholders?
8. What about access to governmental procurement for various stakeholders involved in post production?

9. *What are the gaps in post production systems in the chain and can value chain finance help in redressing any these? If so, how and what must it specifically do to redress the constraints? Can the intervention be practically scaled up after the pilot?*

Appendix 4B

Challenges That Low Income People Face in Rural and Agriculture Livelihood Systems: Issues To Consider While Developing Value Chain Finance Interventions

As noted earlier, value chain finance (VCF) is typically defined as flow of financing within a sub-sector, among various value chain stakeholders, for the specific purpose of getting product (s) to market (s). This is very different from the mere provision of conventional financing, where one of the chain stakeholders (for example, a specific firm/entity and often primary producers) gains access to financial services, independent of other stakeholders. We adopt the broader definition here.

In this appendix, we look at constraints[3] that low income people face in agro and rural enterprises that need to be considered while developing value chain finance interventions:

---

[3] This appendix has been compiled from various resources as also personal experiences. The resources are far too many to acknowledge her but I am grateful to all of them.

- *Challenge # I: Transport Cost to Bring Product to Markets*: Many of these low income people live in remote rural areas or high population low-income urban areas, from where accessing markets is somewhat difficult. Generally, transport costs add a further element to pricing and they seriously limit the competitiveness of the product or service while hampering physical access to the market place and the opportunity to trade locally. Access to affordable and reliable transport is therefore very critical

- *Challenge # II: Lack of Access to Market Intelligence and Such Information:* For many marginal producers, small scale vendors and rural enterprises, their trading is acknowledged only as part of the informal sector; consequently it is invisible, under-reported and un-recorded for the most part. As a consequence, many of them are not registered and therefore have not declared themselves as economic entities and hence, are not recognized as users of market and such information. For example, as vendors or producers or rural enterprises for several years, they would have used their own innate intelligence to recognize trends, but these are un-recorded and part of an oral tradition that does not allow for any type of true and representative trend analysis. In the case of some produce, there are marketing information sources, but the producers are neither aware nor able to consult and use these. In this global economy that is increasingly not adequate. *Hence, access to disaggregated market categories and market information is very critical.*

- *Challenge # III: Inability to Use Market Information in Production:* Without data and information there is little opportunity for the small producers and/or rural enterprises to develop the market trend analysis skills. Further, the skill of using market intelligence information in product development and production planning is also not developed. In addition, without the requisite baselines to create a database and maintain it, it is virtually impossible to generate analysis and trend statements to support business advisory services for these entrepreneurs. The key is therefore to strengthen producer registration and enterprise recording systems, while training producers in the use of marketing information in formal production planning. *Facilitating the development of Business Development Services (BDS) providers is also critical.*

- *Challenge # IV: Product Cost and Quality:* The limited market potential within a limited population generates limited sales that do not stimulate bulk purchasing. Input costs are high and consequently the final product price is not always competitive. Product quality also remains undependable and uncertain. Also, micro/small entrepreneurs and such rural enterprises generally use household grade equipment, implements and utensils in production. Experience indicates that the production environment limits the ability to scale up production to commercial quantities. As a result, customers are forced to find suppliers of better quality. The sole trader or small rural enterprise is faced with a double dilemma often – production is a time consuming operation and she/he has little time for marketing. The demands for quality assurance and the emergence of more competitive producers has also eroded these markets. Local purchasers as well as those involved in preparing produce for export have complained of inconsistent supplies of the albeit high quality produce (especially, rural handicrafts), difficulty to contact the supplier, and inadequate returns policies by the suppliers. Suppliers complain of their inability to provide credit to their purchasers. *Therefore, developing a local quality assurance certification system which linked with strengthened producer registration/enterprise recording systems and improved capability to use of marketing information in formal production planning and the use of Business Development Services (BDS) for operations should help producers/rural enterprises improve product quality and service provision.*

- *Challenge # V: Capital for Cost Effective Production Operations:* Many of the small and micro entrepreneurs have limited access to finance and mostly from either MFIs, cooperatives or informal sector financiers. Mainstream commercial banks are still a rarity, when one looks at the larger picture. The limitation of traditional microcredit in supporting livelihood and productions systems of low income people are well known and need no further emphasis. The alternative is to go to banks but most of these enterprises lack collateral to access the capital for improvements that enhance access to better market linkages and/or improve production. The credit application process is intimidating. Because of poor production and market records, some have little basis for completing the credit application process, and are not able to corroborate details about the business. Lack of literacy is another aspect in this situation. Thus, micro and such rural enterprises lack confidence in a credit system that tends not to favour the small-scale producer. Their operations are considered high risk. As they are credit shy, they have no credit rating as well. *The key would be to develop financial services that are responsive to the peculiarities of their production and livelihood systems – the formal or alternative financial sector need to be incentivized to serve small producers and rural enterprises for their livelihoods. Providing mere consumption loans as in micro-finance is insufficient.*

- *Challenge # VI: Inputs for Production:* Inputs are increasingly costly and their availability is also not stable and this is another aspect that affects small producers and such rural enterprises. There are huge imperfections in the input markets

- *Challenge # VII: Prevalence of Undesirable Marketing Practices:* There are some undesirable marketing practices among small producers and these are:
    ☞ Inconsistent supply and quality within a given period;
    ☞ Lower quality produce being offered at prices equivalent to higher quality produce;

- ☞ Poor handling and packaging of produce;
- ☞ Limited variety of produce offered;
- ☞ In-adequate information on projected supplies available to the purchaser; and
- ☞ Lack of appreciation of and adherence to the purchasing and delivery norms.

The above challenges—in the daily livelihood situations and production of low income people engaged in agriculture and rural enterprises—if not comprehensively addressed, will render any value chain finance intervention sub-optimal in terms of utility and impact. In fact, these challenges are a source of opportunity for Value Chain Finance (VCF) interventions as well in terms of the kind of initiatives to support in the respective chains.

Appendix 5

Note on Copyright Aspects

Ramesh S Arunachalam claims copyright only with the original writings, ideas, interpretation, and analysis done by the author, Ramesh S Arunachalam. No copyright is claimed with regard to any material that is quoted, which are any ways, very negligible. Furthermore, where quoted, material that is quoted has been paraphrased and cited appropriately—such quotes, which are negligible in comparative terms to the overall book, would anyways come under fair use policy. Where original quotes are used, they are primarily taken from Statutory Enquiry Commissions. All of these, to the best of my understanding and interpretation of the law, are free of copyright protection. In fact, as per the website of the Office of the Law Revision Counsel United States Code[4] and the website of the United States Copyright office,[5] as per Section, 105,. (Subject matter of copyright: United States Government works), copyright protection (under this title) is not available for any work of the United States Government.

---

[4] Office of the Law Revision Counsel United States Code, 17 USC: Subject Matter of Copyright: United States Government works, http://uscode.house.gov/view.xhtml?req=%28title:17%20section:105%20edition:prelim%29

[5] Copyright Law of the United States of America and Related Laws Contained in Title 17 of the *United States Code*, Section 105, Subject Matter of Copyright: United States Government works, http://www.copyright.gov/title17/92chap1.html#105

That said, every document that has been quoted has been thoroughly checked for copyright information and none of the documents from which quotes have been taken contain copyright notice either as a symbol © (the letter C in a circle), or the word "Copyright," or the abbreviation "Copr."

There is no name of the owner, no abbreviation by which the name can be recognized, no generally known alternative designation of the owner, nor any indication of an owner of any copyright in these government works. Therefore, in the absence of the copyright notice and copyright owner information and as per Sections 105 and 403 of the Copyright Laws of the United States, it can only be inferred that these government reports, orders, releases etc. (representing work of the United States federal government), are not protected by copyright. Likewise, the concerned websites have either stated that "information on State Department websites is in the public domain and may be copied and distributed without permission,"[6] or they have stated that "all of the content of the website constitutes a work of the United States federal government under sections 105[7] and 403[8] of title 17 of the U.S. Code," which again frees the information from copyright protection.

---

[6] U.S. Department of State, Copyright Information, http://www.state.gov/misc/87529.htm#copyright

[7] Subject Matter of Copyright: United States Government works, U.S Code 105.

[8] Copyright Law of the United States of America and Related Laws Contained in Title 17 of the *United States Code,* Section 403, Notice of copyright: Publications incorporating United States Government works, http://www.copyright.gov/title17/92chap4.html

Powering A Billion Dreams

About the Author

Ramesh S Arunachalam wears many hats. He is an Industrial Engineer from the National Institute of Technology (NIT), Trichy, India and an MBA (with Dual Concentration, Strategy and Marketing) from the Carlson School of Management, University of Minnesota, Minneapolis, USA. In the last 30 years, he has been a columnist with the Hindu Business Line (1995-97) and Moneylife (2011-2013), a development practitioner and strategic advisor. He has worked in a wide range of areas including financial sector regulation and supervision, financial inclusion, microfinance, livelihoods and MSMEs, Gender and microfinance, ERP systems for microfinance and infrastructure finance, urban development, infrastructure financing, GIS for urban planning and e Governance.

During the last 30 years, Ramesh has completed over 260 professional assignments. He has worked in 570 districts of India and has also travelled and worked extensively in over 25 countries in North America, Asia, Africa, Europe and the Caribbean across diverse projects (in senior positions). He is passionate about his work and brings strong inter-disciplinary insight to his assignments. His clients include governments (Governments of India, St Lucia, Singapore, Malawi, Uganda, Philippines, Afghanistan etc, several State Governments in India and many GoI Institutions like NCRPB, SIDBI, NABARD etc), bi-lateral agencies (DFID, USAID, DANIDA, NORAD, SIDA etc), multi-lateral agencies (UNDP, World Bank, ADB, IFAD, The Commonwealth Secretariat etc), regulators, commercial banks, investment banks, microfinance institutions, private sector firms and several other stakeholders globally.

He has authored numerous reports/studies/papers as part of his assignments, several of which have been published internationally and received global recognition. His blog on microfinance has been well received and he has also penned two books in microfinance and financial inclusion—**The Journey of Indian Microfinance: Lessons for the Future** and **An Idea Which Went Wrong: Commercial Microfinance in India**—both of which have received critical acclaim. His first novel is an entertaining crime thriller—**Where Angels Prey**—released in April 2015 through AuthorsUpFront, which again was well received. His non-fiction writing continued with critically acclaimed popular books—**"Madam President: History in the Making?"**, **"Dirty Money: The U.S. Presidential Elections 2016"**, **"The Cinderella Notes: Demonitization and The Indian Economy"** and **"9/11: The Unanswered Questions"** (see www.amazon.com).

Title – **Where Angels Prey**
Author – Ramesh S Arunachalam
Size – 5.5 inches × 8.5 inches
No of Pages – 204
Binding – Paperback
ISBN – 978-9384439378

While the rest of the world reels under a severe financial crisis, India's microfinance sector enjoys an unprecedented boom. Why on earth are people investing such huge amounts of money in an obscure industry, especially at the time of global recession? And why is Wall Street suddenly so interested in India's poor?

That is exactly what Robert Bradlee, senior correspondent with *The New York Post*, sets off to investigate, along with his journalist friend, Chandresh. Little does he know that his search for a scoop would lead him through a complex multi-pronged web of deceit, fraud, manipulation and financial crime, remote controlled from distant lands by an entire chain of financial sector stakeholders.

Gripping, racy and meticulously researched, this financial thriller weaves in and out of the affluent world of high-powered boardrooms and the gruelling poverty of the remotest villages of India, to reveal the devastating truths that often lurk behind "good intentions".

www.ingramcontent.com/pod-product-compliance
Lightning Source LLC
Chambersburg PA
CBHW031610210526
45464CB00004B/1515